AGAINST
All Odds

AGAINST
All Odds

DR. SIMON GEORGE TAUKENI

PARTRIDGE

To order additional copies of this book, contact
Toll Free 0800 990 914 (South Africa)
+44 20 3014 3997 (outside South Africa)
orders.africa@partridgepublishing.com

www.partridgepublishing.com/africa

CONTENTS

This is a true life story of an ordinary poor orphan and a Namibian refugee boy who did extraordinary things in a normal and amazing way. A life of a poor village boy who did supernatural things with a simple smile.

DEDICATION

I dedicate this book to my late parents and everyone who has supported me in my life journey. To the Orphans and Other Vulnerable Children of the World this book is for you.

ACKNOWLEDGEMENT

To my father and mother thank you for giving me life. Great grandmother, my step mother, volunteers in Swapo Refugee Camps in both Kwanza-Sul, Angola and Nyango, Zambia, my teachers and professors, project supervisor Professor Rembe, thank you for shaping my life. I thank the orphans and other vulnerable children that shared their time with me as source of inspiration when I was busy writing this book. My dear colleagues at many places I worked, I thank you for your support towards my life. Last but not least, my best friends: Prof. Maree, Victoria, Everlyne and Zoleka who believed in my idea to publish my story, thank you guys for your support. My words of gratitude further go to Meme Esther Ndinelao Nghipandwa for her valuable support towards my book. All glory to God, Almighty.

KEY LOCAL TERMS AND ENGLISH TRANSLATION

Evanda: A common Oshiwambo cultural dried green leaves that grow in the fields during the rainy season

Meekulu: Grandmother or great grandmother or an elderly female person

Meme: A biological mother or an adult woman

Mukwamalanga: A totem type

Nautoni: A place where people lost their lives

Omahangu: Wheat

Ombidi: An Oshiwambo fresh and cooked green leaves that grow in the field during the rainy season

Omufima: A fountain

Ondobe: A pond

Ondungu: A well

Ongubu: A traditional fence made out of wood

Oshifima: A porridge

Otombo: Home brewed common drink

Tate: A biological father or an adult man

Tatekulu: Grandfather or great grandfather or an elderly male person

Shiti: A nickname given to someone who has a passion to work in the wood

MY FIRST WORDS

Life is described by many people as a journey. For me it is a journey that has a beginning and an end to it. The first step of one's life journey begins the day of birth and ends the day of death. My belief is that after death there is a final destination, where some lives will go to Heaven and some of evil lives will go to Hell. Looking at my life as I write this book I deserve to go to Heaven and God promised me that I will. Read for yourself things I had to go through in life as I work day and night to fulfill my God given assignments.

Let me now give you the overview of what to expect in this book and why it is a MUST read. My very first words to you is that if I am one of you perhaps you are a parent who has children like me, remember that one day soon or later we will die and our children will become orphans. It is therefore important that you get a copy of this book as a gift to your children for inspiration and hope. Or perhaps you are a village person like me and struggled to survive and yet you managed to achieve your goals, this book is very good for you as a reminder of how poor village men and women can work hard to become successful. Please keep in mind that this book is written by a poor village person like you.

Or perhaps you were in a refugee camp say for example you were born or grew up in exile during Namibia's liberation struggle as a refugee child like me and life has been tough for you and you wanted to give up please take time to read this book, I promise it will touch you and change your life for the better. Or perhaps like me, your parents died and even all your grandparents and everybody else significant in your family died and you were left all alone with no hope for a better future. You must read my story to see for yourself that you are not alone. God will send His Angels to support you in your journey of life, just like He did for me and He still continues lining up people to support me. Or perhaps you grew up poor with little family support and you failed to get the support at the time you needed it the most, this book can teach you that

1

anything and everything is possible. Perhaps you are working with orphans and other less privileged people in your community like what I do, you may want to share my story to them and please do it without fear.

Everything I wrote in this book came from my personal life experiences. I wrote genuinely straight from my heart, mind and soul. When I was about to start writing I made a promise to myself that let me be just me and tell my story in the manner that represent me and my character. You know *mos* I am calm, funny sometimes, loving, kind and honest poor orphan boy.

I know very well that some of you readers will wake up at night to read this book over and over again. I know for sure that some of you will read my story from time to time because I am a humorous person. I also know that many of you who happen to know less of me and quick to judge me without a clear understanding of where I came from, you will look at me differently and appreciate me even better after reading my story. Some of you will be shocked and you will go like: Ooh poor boy really? Or something like: Oh My God really George went through that hardship and many more surprises.

But remember that everyone has a story to tell and it is now my turn to tell mine. The fact that you pick this book makes me believe that you too are on your journey to start writing yours in a book like me. To tell you the truth writing this book has been the most exciting thing ever and a healing process. This book made me face my good and bad past, my joyful memories as well as my fears. It definitely took me down memory lane! I now offer this book to you in anticipation that it will give you healing, inspiration and hope. Whenever you find something more interesting which I know you will, don't hold back just laugh out loud and where you may feel like crying don't hold your tears, release them they will bring healing to your heart. Enjoy my life story.

BACK TO MY ROOTS

Going back to my roots and memory lane comes with deep emotions of sorrow and a great sense of loss. Nonetheless to say, I like to tell you briefly about my family tree. I was born by the man who is my hero and a true brave father George Mandume Taukeni. I have six siblings; four paternal brothers, a sister and one maternal sister. I have two sisters. My father was born as a King with his twin sister my lovely aunt Tuyeimo Kaleinasho Taukeni. They have one paternal brother my uncle Laurentius Gabriel Taukeni. My father's parents were late Gabriel Taukeni and Ottilie Tuutale Ndilimeke Leevi. I never had a chance to meet grandmother Ottilie, she died long before I was born. She left too soon, leaving her children, my father and aunt too young to be without a mother.

My grandfather's mother is late Eunike *Mukwamalanga* Mokaxwa. In our culture, elder women are known by their totem, therefore she was called *meekulu Mukwamalanga*. *Meekulu Mukwamalanga* had two sons; my late grandfather Gabriel Taukeni and Aron Hafeni. My late grandfather Gabriel Taukeni's father was Cotlieb Taukeni. Cotlieb Taukeni was one of the headmen of Omundudu village which also happens to be my birthplace. My father, grandfather, great grandparents (my grandfather's parents) all lived, died and are buried in the village of Omundudu. This is the village where the roots of my paternal family tree are found and sustained. That is a brief story of my paternal family roots on my right hand.

On my left hand are my maternal family roots. I shall first start talking about my late mother, the queen of my heart. My mother is Maria Mwaifanange Kalola. She had only one sister from her maternal side, my late aunt Saima Hangula- Nghinamito. My dear late mother had two brothers, my uncles: late Shini, and Mwaetako. My closest maternal uncle was the late Mwaetako. He was a good hearted man and a family man at heart.

My late grandmother is better known as *Meekulu* Ottilie Mukwamani. I should confess that I did not get the opportunity to know my mother's paternal family, the Kalola family. I did not even meet my maternal grandfather face to face before he passed on. My mother told me that my grandfather was taller and slender like me. He was living in the village called Omunghete near Omungwelume. I know very well that my family roots are bigger and longer, I only focused on the immediate close families. I apologize if I left to mention some of my family roots which are equally important. The focus of my book is also not to dig too deep due to lack of knowledge on my part. However, my children and children of my children will somehow get a picture of who my parents were. Let us now read about my birth and growing up.

My birth and growing up

This section is unpacking step by step my life from the day my parents met to plant the seed to the very day my mother gave birth to me. It unpacks my childhood experiences as a little boy with my great grandmother at our village. It also covers the time I left my great grandmother to live with my father after he got married. This is my life story and hopefully many people from all generations will continue to talk about for years to come. I wish to express that I cherish all the moments I experienced growing up from the time I was born and how I grew up.

This is how my story started leading to my birth day. I am not too sure if my father knew that one day he would give life to a boy like me. Did he dream about that son, not sure he did. I just discovered the truth after I spoke to my father. The truth is that my father never planned to have a son called Simon George, meaning me. He was just an innocent young school boy playing with life and life ended up too big and too serious for him. He was surprised to discover that my mother was expecting his child. He was very surprised, it is true he was. Please don't argue with me I know what I am talking about. I spoke with my father almost the whole day in Walvis Bay town, at our second home. We were in our small warm sitting room relaxing on Sunday and there was a radio playing good gospel songs on the background. I could see my dear dad was in a very good mood to open up to me.

Believe me I had this question in my heart for a long time, and I seized the chance to ask my dear dad how I was born and to make him talk of my birth while he was in this good mood. When I say my dad was in a good mood I do not mean he was under the influence or anything unusual, that he did not know what he was talking about. No! Even though my father was generally a happy person, funny and loving all the time, that day he was a very special man.

I asked my father to tell me how he met my mother. This is how I started: Dad I have been with this personal question and it is something I need to know if you can help me. He smiled like he already knew that I wanted to open some pages of his past. When I saw him smiling I was praying inside my heart that, dad you must tell me all about it.

He asked me what it was and I said: Dad please tell me how you met my mother and the two of you to bring me in this world? Mmhm…he first laughed and wanted to change the subject. I was so convinced that I would not leave my dad alone without getting to the bottom of how he met my poor mother. I think when he realized that I was serious and I needed to know the hidden truth he smiled again and said, ok son I will tell you. He said that he knew I might not like what I was about to hear but that was the truth of how he met my mother.

He started by saying that after he completed Form 5 at Omundudu Combined School he went to continue his education, Form 6 at Omungwelume. He could not walk every day from Omundudu to Omungwelume for schooling due to the long distance. He had to find a place to stay near the school. He was fortunate because he had a family relative his uncle Joseph Mokaxwa who had a house around Omungwelume area. There was no better place for him to stay than with his uncle Mokaxwa, since he was brought up and taken care of by Eunike Mokaxwa our great grandmother. Grandmother Eunike and Joseph were brother and sister. But *Tate* Joseph was a man who was married to Saima, my aunt (my mother's sister). That time my mother was living with her sister in the same house.

The moment he mentioned that he and my mother were in the same house I almost shouted, stop it dad I got it! He then revealed that he and my mother met there just once and before anyone noticed what had happened, the seed was already planted. He said they never had a love affair between them since they were regarded as a brother and sister in the same house. He explained that it was news from my mother to her sister that she was pregnant and George was responsible.

The news angered my aunt Saima so much that she chased her sister, my mother out of the house. My mother then went to live with her mother *Meekulu Mukwamani* in Ongobeyaola. I was looking at my father when he was telling me the painful experience my mother had endured. I asked what happened to him after my mother was chased out of the house and whether he stayed behind to complete his education. He said he did stay behind to complete his education but life in the house was not the same anymore. His uncle was challenging him from time to time asking what he would do to the child and the poor mother. He promised his uncle that he would take full responsibility of taking care of me, he even jokingly said "That's why you are here with me, it was because of that promise I made to take care of you even before you were born". We laughed out loud about that.

What a day it was with my father. We started talking in the morning then in the afternoon until in the evening. I remember my dad talking to me on the same subject while preparing for our lunch and even during lunch. I was even still teasing him while I was washing the dishes saying he was somewhat a naughty boy. I was really hard on my dad. It was a special date with the man who brought me to this world. It was a discussion that went even on throughout the night until I slept without knowing how I slept.

I wrote down the date in my notebook titled: a date with my father on Sunday March 12, 1995. After my father had answered my personal old question satisfactorily I felt so happy and relieved. It is true that truth pains but it is also true that truth heals. I truly felt good and totally satisfied after my dad had opened his past life to tell me without fear about how my life began. Even though they are both dead and gone, at least I know the truth about how my life began and I thanked my father for being kind to tell me the honest truth.

The question about the day I was born I had the privilege to ask my late maternal grandmother. I was about 18 years old when I asked her to tell me if she knew anything about my birth day. If I could remember very well that time I was at Eengendjo Secondary School and I needed a letter from my church to receive Holy Communion from a nearby church. After I was given a letter from the Ongenga Elcin Church I discovered that I was baptized on the same day I was born. It was an unusual thing to happen so I was curious to find out more about what exactly happened. To tell the truth I have been always this curious boy, asking tough questions and I never knew that one day I would need to write this book about my life.

What I learned from my maternal grandmother *Mukwamani* before she passed on was that my birth day was unpredictable, they never imagined that I would survive it. I was born on the 23rd of December 1973 and it was also my baptism day. My maternal grandmother revealed then to me that my mother gave birth to me at home and chances were higher that I would not survive, that's why they had to ask a church representative to baptize me. I was baptized as Simon George, my childhood names.

Apparently, those who were around the day I was born asked where my father was. Then my mother told them that he was not there and his name was George. So they agreed to add the name George to my name thinking that my father could have another name that I was supposed to be baptized with. That was how I became known as Simon George. In our culture a father of the child is responsible to give a name that the child would be baptized with. Then I was born and I started to grow up.

Growing up as a child was not a normal exciting journey. My childhood was dramatic, funny and full of responsibilities. I started taking many responsibilities at a time I was still a baby. I learned too then from my grandmother that my mother was not always healthy from the time I was a baby. Therefore when I was three years old my father had sent for me to live with him and my paternal great grandmother Eunike in Omundudu village. By then my father, uncle Aron and I were all living with our grandmother and I was a child of the house. Uncle Aron is the son of my grandfather Hafeni. My father was always away from home working far in Oranjemund. Oranjemund is one of the Namibian diamond towns. He was only home once a year usually during Christmas.

Like most poor village children, I started growing up so fast, doing so many household chores namely collecting firewood, fetching water, cleaning the house and learning to cook. Things were happening very fast and yet I was still a child just at a tender age of three years. Luckily I had a great teacher from home my great grandmother. She taught me how best I could be doing my house chores. She was really a greater teacher. Due to her old age my great grandmother could not do much for our beautiful small home. She was only playing a supervisory role making sure that she reminded me that there was water, firewood and *omahangu* that is flour to cook our porridge.

I was the only child at home playing both the roles of a boy and a girl child at the same time. I could tell life was very tough for us. Small as I was I could clearly feel the poverty all around us, from lack of food, clothes and blankets. I learned earlier in my life to be thankful and content with little we had in our small home. In most cases I depended on the palm fruits and other God given natural fruits that were available for free. I also used my bow and arrows to bring meat especially bird's meat home.

I knew exactly that we were poor but I never used our poverty situation as an excuse to commit crime like stealing other people's things. I never liked taking anything that did not belong to me. My great grandmother taught me that I should never leave home to go and steal because we are poor. I never understood where we depended on for survival. Yes I can say that my great grandmother's pension was helping us a lot. I think we were lucky because my grandmother was not addicted to alcohol. It was therefore easy for us to spend our grandmother's pension only on foodstuff and other basic family needs.

I remember one day when my great grandmother asked me to take her to one of our neighbor's house and I was aware she went to borrow. I came to learn that whenever that happened, and great grandmother had to borrow, the situation was beyond all her means. She was very strong and full of ideas to survive. She even taught me to use boiled water and salt when there was no dried spinach commonly known as *evanda* or anything to serve with our porridge especially in dry season. However, during the rainy season we were blessed with a number of choices of foodstuff ranging from fresh products such as, spinach, tomatoes, *ombidi, omundjulu, evanda* to name just a few. We had also fish, frogs and tortoise in the water ponds that we could use to make our delicious meal at home. I loved rainy season!

Nevertheless to say, our home was very peaceful and full of love. Our great grandmother never raised her voice or her hand to us as a family. She was very caring, loving and understanding. When I was lonely I turned to my great grandmother because she was a very good story teller. I remember her sharing stories about when she was a young beautiful girl. And her story when she was married by a tough head man Cottlieb, my great grandpa. Apparently my great grandpa had promised to give her the very best in the world and even the entire Omundudu village would be in her hand if my great grandma would just marry him. That was my great grandpa's proposal, it was funny, and romantic. Whenever my great grandma recounted that proposal I could see the excitement in her eyes. I thought they were truly in love. We used to remind each other about that proposal a lot of times. My great grandma had a really wonderful sense of humor.

I also joined uncle Aron and his friends who used to come home to play some traditional games. We played games called *owela*, battery throwing game and bottle tops game. Believe me as young as I was, I was the most difficult opponent to beat. I quickly mastered most of the games and I developed my skills exceptionally well.

A day I will never forget ever, was when my uncle Aron was challenging me in a battering throwing game. There were some other family relatives from my grandpa's house; Leena and Auguste watching our game. My problem was if I happened to win the game I would bully the loser without showing any sign of respect. I could roll on the ground laughing and boasting that I was the best and all that irritating behavior. That day we played a total of three games, which I won them all without mercy or anything for my poor uncle to take home.

The battery throwing game was very simple with simple rules. It was actually to throw a battery so that it rolls and hits down all the batteries of your opponent. The first person to hit down all the batteries was regarded as a winner. At the time I hit nearly all his batteries down and I was only left with two batteries to hit before I became a winner for the third consecutive time, my uncle became very angry. Leena and Auguste who were watching became my cheer leaders and they made it even worse for him. A situation that made my uncle very angry, losing to a small boy. From that incident I never tried to play with him any game at home even though I was also to blame for being a bully.

Despite the fact that my father was in the same house he was always away with work. But when he came home for Christmas holiday we all used to be happy. He normally brought everyone clothes, shoes and food for the house. After he got married in 1981 he stayed only two years before he went to build his home with the new family.

I stayed behind to continue taking care of our great grandmother. Luckily he made his home in the same village not far from his grandmother. One year after they had left us I should admit that life was not the same, I stopped going to school as I used to and my father was not happy about me not going to school regularly. It was then he decided that I should come over to stay with him. Leaving my great grandmother was also not easy at all but staying would put my future in danger. I therefore decided to go and stay with my father.

That was my experience living with my great grandmother from the age of three years until when I was about ten years old.

Living with my father and step mother in my new home was a pleasant experience. I was finally discharged from doing many house chores all by myself. In my new home there were girls Saima and Vilma who were mature enough to take care of the cooking, pounding and collecting firewood. We only shared other chores like fetching water, cultivating and cleaning the house. We had also a domestic worker who was mainly taking care of my little brother Appollos by then. I still recall how she was feeding my cute small brother abnormally. That boy could finish the whole container of milk powder in a single week. He was a big and fat boy, I never saw anyone picking up Appollos throwing him in the air as most people do with small children. I also could not remember anyone of the family giving him a piggyback for a period of one hour long, some took five minutes and many less than two. He was huge and he still is. Sorry boy I am being hard on you now.

Let me also I admit my sins and ask for forgiveness because my baby brother and I were sharing the milk powder behind the scenes and spoilt my step mother's budget. I think I enjoyed the taste and I could not stop feeding myself. I think God will forgive me since my mother was a poor woman, I never got a chance to get such privileges like milk powders. No! It was not stealing I know what you are thinking it was only an opportunity for me to get multivitamins and minerals for my normal growth and development while there was nobody watching and stopping me. Promise me you will only read it here and leave it here you are not going to tell my step mother.

Nearly everything was good in my new home and I was somehow living a completely different life. There was only one common problem facing our entire village when I was a small boy. Our village faced a serious water scarcity and drought. Both human beings and animals were negatively affected. We depended solely on water boreholes, wells and ponds. Especially during summer season we used to suffer a lot.

As an intervention measure, neighbors used to wake up early in the morning to go and dig their wells at Eemwele village in Oshana, better known as *Onaifide* which was about 1.5 kilometers away from home. That was the toughest time working on the wells. We were like people working in the mines digging for diamonds. We dug and dug to find water and when we finally found it we used to rejoice and celebrate. I still remember waking up early in the morning riding a bicycle with two water containers, one in front and the other one on the back of my bicycle. In between there was sand soil at Omangela village where I could not ride my bicycle, instead I used to push my bicycle with two water containers, they were too heavy to push on that sand. When there was something wrong with the bicycle I used to carry a bucket of water on my head. I am still wondering why I did not become a short man after carrying a lot of buckets on my head during those tough times. Overall that was part of growing up in the village as well as part of doing normal domestic chores. I think I am proud of myself for having gone through that hardship. Sometimes I think it contributed to the type of a man that I am today.

There were many positive things happening in my life too especially in school work. I also started doing very well in school. I remember the same year I went to my father's home, my step mother used to help me with my homework and school work. By the end of that year I became the second best learner in grade 3. In addition, there were many good family rituals I liked most when I came to live with my father.

One of those family rituals I enjoyed most was doing evening prayers. After every evening meal we used to gather as a family in the sitting room for the evening prayer. I enjoyed how we used to sing together. There was a rooster where everyone had a chance to conduct the evening prayer regardless how small or big we were. It was beautiful.

I also enjoyed Christmas day at home very much. Our home during Christmas day was ever filled with good food and music. We had a big radio with a tape recorder at home and I used to be a DJ playing my favorite country music. It was incredible, I liked to sing along as well. Many children from the neighboring homes used to come to our home during Christmas night to dance and listen to good music.

Notably to say, I was always lucky because my step mother made sure I had new clothes and shoes for Christmas. She was really kind to me during Christmas and New Year. It was also the time my father used to come home for his annual holiday, bringing us new clothes and lots and lots of sweets. My father being a kind hearted man and most famous in the village, whenever he was around our home was always flooded by people coming in and out to see him. I remember some poor village men usually getting clothes and shoes from my father. I was admiring him how he was treating the poor people in our village. I just wanted to be like my father when I was growing up, he was a very kind man.

Some of the school holidays my father made an effort to invite us to his work in Oranjemund town. When I had a chance to spend my holiday in Oranjemund it was out of this world experience. It was a wonderful place to be. There was an entertainment center with sporting activities to play with. My best game was snooker and squash. Whenever it was lunch time the dining hall was always open to everyone to eat as much as he or she wished. Nearly everyone who was in Oranjemund was overweight because of free good food and biscuits offered in the dining hall. I also met one of my best friend Katemba who was working there. He used to take me out to have fun. We used to go for fishing at the sea on Saturday and sometimes Sunday mornings. Spending my school holiday in Oranjemund was the highlight of my childhood.

Generally speaking living with my father and step mother has shaped my life in many different dimensions. I was about ten years when I came to live with my father and I left shortly for exile in Angola and Zambia respectively at the age of thirteen years. I returned back home from exile at the age of seventeen. After I returned from exile we continued living happily in our home. By then I was admitted in the school hostel, I only used to come home during school holidays.

I spent most of my time at home writing my stories and playing soccer with small boys from our village. Since there were many boys who used to come to our home because my father and step mother usually bought us soccer balls to keep ourselves busy I then decided to form a football club called Future Boys. We started up a team and we trained very well. It was a team which was full of small boys but we used to win many games. It was a good team. I nicknamed every boy playing for Future Boys Club, some of the names were: Moloi, Dr, Fizi, Masinga, Omo, late Troublemaker, Maradona, Danger, Blackboy, Dedele, Pelle, Wiseman and many others. They are still well known by these names. We involved most of our parents as advisory board members. I remember *Meme* Ndamononghenda was our treasurer, a finance minister. When there were tournaments we used to ask her for some money to pay for the tournament. After winning, all of us we ran as a team to her house and we gave her our prize money to save for the team. She was very good to us, she knew that we truly respected and loved her as our dear mother.

I can honestly say I spent my childhood and teenage years with a great family. There were many good things and family rituals I would recommend for my own family. Number one example I could write down was the love we shared as a family through singing together during evening prayers, really that one was the most powerful lesson I learned, the love of the family.

The support my parents gave me in the form of food to eat and not to starve, warm shelter with blankets and bed sheets to survive from cold, clothes and shoes to wear especially during Christmas and New Year. I cannot thank enough my step mother for supporting me with my school needs, she really tried her level best so that I could get my education especially in primary and secondary schools. I thank her from bottom of my heart for all her support. I stayed with my father, step mother and siblings from 1983 until 2000 when my father died. I miss my family so much because it was them that shaped me and prayed for me in my life journey.

Our borehole and Namutoni ponds

I would like to talk about one of the boreholes which became part of my life story in many ways. The borehole whose picture is attached below was constructed before Namibia's independence to provide water to school community. It is therefore situated in close proximity to the village school called Omundudu Combined School. School children in those days used to call it *Shiteengela*. I did not know where the name came from but everyone called it *Shiteengela*. Even though it was constructed to serve the school community only it ended up supplying water to the entire village and nearby surroundings like Omangela village too.

Let me now write why *Shiteengela* became part of my life journey and why I had to include it in my book. This borehole became part of my story in two ways. First of all, when I was a small boy living with my great grandmother the only place I fetched water from was this borehole. I fetched water day and night from it. I only came to know and use it after it was already broken where two people used to assist one another. One would stay outside to take out the bucket and the other person would be inside to fill up the bucket.

After the bucket was full the person inside would shout to remind the one outside that the bucket was full so that he or she could take it out and so on. The borehole was very deep and many a times there were broken bottles thrown in it. It has steps to use as one gets in and out. Since the borehole was serving our two villages, there were always people to help one another by drawing water in order to fill up all the buckets and containers.

In the event where there was nobody to assist me I used to go inside with my bucket, filled it with water and then I would put it on my head while my hands were on the steps moving up. The bucket used to be on my head without any support, the only support was my stiff neck to keep it standing on my head without falling. At the beginning, the bucket used to fall, I started using one hand on the bucket while the other hand was on the steps to help me moving up. I was very young when I was doing all these things. When I reflect on how I used to get water from this borehole, sometimes even in the evening just thinking about it, my head starts spinning. I think I was a very resilient child throughout my childhood. I learned to do many things on my own at a very tender age, but truly, did I have a choice not to do things alone by then? Not really, being the only child at home I did not have any better choice but simply to carry out my duties independently and confidently.

The second reason why *Shiteengela* become part of my story was that I nearly lost my life in this borehole. I fell in it many times and I survived. The last incident was deadly, I only survived by the power of God. I lost a lot of blood until I became unconscious. I found myself lying in a hospital bed not knowing how I got there. It was very bad but I thanked God for giving me a second chance to live. There are still many scares on my head as a result of this borehole. The incident happened because as school children, we were very naughty, we used to play dangerous games inside the borehole, such as competing on the steps to see who was faster to get inside it first. We played many dangerous games there.

During the last incident, many people who had witnessed the incident did not believe I could come out alive. After that incident every time people saw me they would ask me so many questions as to how I survived and warned me not to go near the borehole ever again. I believed them to stay away from it. It was only now that I revisited the place when I went to take pictures for the book. I would also like to remind the people especially the teachers and parents to keep an eye on children and stopping them from going to play there.

Next to the borehole were many ponds made by community people as source of water. Sometimes local people referred to the ponds as going to fetch water from Nautoni. The name Nautoni came about because there were people who drowned and lost their lives in one of the ponds. The first unfortunate incident was when a young woman from the village fell into it and drowned. I heard from our community elders that her friend who had witnessed the incident could not save her due to deep waters. She however ran to the nearby house to inform people that her friend had fallen into the water and they should rush there to save her. When they came she had unfortunately lost her life already. That was how Namutoni came into being. Namutoni is a name in Oshikwanyama dialect to refer to the place where many people lost their lives.

Picture 1: Omundudu borehole

Kandjedje thorn tree and the pond

The story of my life cannot be written without the mentioning of Kandjedje thorn tree and the pond. From my research about the origin of the name Kandjedje, some of the elders I consulted agreed on the origin of the name. They revealed that the name Kandjedje came about when some of the women from the village were catching fish in the pond. One of them had a damaged traditional necklace known in Oshikwanyama as *oshindjedja* that she wore on her waist. It spread all over in the water. By then these women were looking for it saying where was *oshindjedja*? That was how the name Kandjedje came into effect.

Kandjedje became part of my life for three main reasons. First of all, it provided me with a good hunting spot so that we could have meat when I used to shoot down those innocent and yet delicious birds for my family feast. You must believe me that I used to be a sharp shooter and incredible hunter. The tree attracted many birds who used to come drinking water at the pond. My great grandmother was very proud of me. She would tell me that there was nothing in the house to serve with our traditional porridge better known as *oshifima* so I should go out there with my bow and arrows to do what I used to do best shooting birds down.

I remember there were times when it was very cold, I used to bring the fire along from home inside the tree for warmth while I was waiting for the birds to come. Sometimes if it happened that I shot many birds, I started a small braai inside the tree to reward myself for a good hunting well done. It served more like a starter before I went home to prepare the main course. I was a poor village boy but not so poor to enjoy my meat after shooting down the birds. This is why I love listening to my favorite singer Dolly Parton especially one of her hit songs the Coat of Many Colors, "One is only poor if only they choose to be," these are true words.

The second reason and equally important is that Kandjedje pond was my swimming pool. As a poor boy living in the village there was no better place to develop my swimming skills than at Kandjedje pond. It was very popular in our village. For us the small poor village boys and girls it was the only swimming pool we had. Even though our head men and other elders in the village did not like us swimming there because they thought that we were just playing with water. It is only now that I realize that those elders were on our side thinking that we could drown and die in the deep waters of Kandjedje pond. They were doing it for our own safety.

The funny thing I could remember that time was that our elders really spoilt our fun. When we were swimming we could not enjoy it to the fullest because of fear of the elders to chase us out and beat us for playing with water. We had a fear of them coming after us. We used to enjoy swimming there but we used to keep one eye open to see who was coming after us. I vividly recall more than one occasion when the elders came and caught us without us seeing them coming. They used to take our old pants and dirty t-shirt with pigeon holes on them and hide them. We came out of water naked calling on their mercy and begging for forgiveness to bring back our clothes. It was bad experience and yet hilarious. It was like watching a comedy show where we were the main actors, naked running up and down looking for our missing clothes.

Overall Kandjedje pond helped me to develop my swimming skills that enabled me to even score good grades in swimming lessons at the University of Namibia. I got a certificate in swimming during my studies at UNAM, all credit to Kandjedje pond.

The third and the last reason is that Kandjedje was our source of water for family use during the rainy season. When we needed water for washing, cooking and drinking, Kandjedje was the best place to go. Luckily for us it was on our side because it was very close to our home. When it was raining we felt more like we had a tap inside our small home by then.

I took this picture at the time I was writing this book and looking at both the thorn tree and the pond one could see that nothing much has changed, it was just like yesterday. The view just brought my best memories of yesteryears when I was a small boy using the tree and the pond. I thank God for this wonderful creation in my late great grandmother's door step and for our poor village boys and girls to have fun. What a wonderful blessing to our village!

Picture 2: Kandjedje Pond and thorn trees

MY FIRST YEARS
OF SCHOOLING

This section opens up doors to my first years of primary education. That was where all the fun began, indeed school is fun. January 1981 was the year I first started going to school. My first school I attended was Omundudu Combined School situated in our beautiful village. I was eight years old when I started learning how to read and write in what was called Sub-A and my class teacher was Ms. Saara. Our class teacher who was better known to us as *Mee Saara* was a lovely hard working teacher. She was the best mother to all of us.

My favorite grade at Omundudu was Standard 1 with our class teacher Mr. Nakamhela. As a class we had great respect for our class teacher, he was down to earth and he was very good at teaching. I knew he did not spend most of his teaching time in class but whenever he was with us he did his best. He was teaching us English and Environmental Studies.

I was a very obedient student and naughty at times but I was loved by many people. I was a lovable child all my life, from my peers, teachers and *memes who* used to sell fat cakes and *Oshikundu* at school, they all loved me. I was always referred to as *Okaana ka* George, meaning George's child. I enjoyed my time at school. My friends and I had a lot of fun at school. We liked climbing trees to pick fruits. We also had a game called *"A Touch"* where we used to climb trees and jumped from one branch to the next to avoid being given *"A Touch"*.

Also, we usually held a fist fight popular known in Oshikwanyama as *Onghandeka* or *Ondambo*. That game was particularly organized on the last day following the school holiday. It was a fist to fist fight. The game was organized in the same way as a boxing match. First it was the juniors that had to start fighting each other. Usually, a boy used to go in a big circle and whoever wanted to fight him as a challenger would go in the center and if the one found in the center was willing then they would start the fight. If he was afraid he would leave the center until there would be somebody else perhaps of the same age who could challenge to fight. I usually enjoyed watching big boys fighting each other. It was always deadly and bloody.

Even though most teachers at our school did not like the idea of us fighting each other it was seen as part of our culture to groom a boy child into a man. I too fought some boys of my age and I am proud to say that I won most of my fights. I was only beaten one day in my left eye, that was very bad and the crowd stopped the fight. The good thing about fist fighting was that if it was seen that one of the boys was beaten badly the big boys had to stop the fight. One was never left beaten until death or serious injury. It was a fight yet it was just a game.

Omundudu Combined School will always have a special place in my heart since it was where I first learned how to read and write. I think with my personality I never really had steady friends for sure at school. I was playing and walking with anybody and everybody. For the purpose of this book about my life I can mention some of my friends at Omundudu CS as follows: Heiki, Timo, Titus, Edward, and Erven. I left Omundudu Combined School in 1988 for exile while I was in Standard 4.

GOING INTO EXILE

The year was 1987 when the idea came to cross the borders in order to join other Namibians who were in exile for the liberation of our country. We were five guys, and I was the youngest of all the boys in the group to cross the border into Angolan soil. Among us was one of the People Liberation Army of Namibia (PLAN) fighter who was leading us the way. The first day we planned to join the liberation struggle was ruined because the family of the other three guys in the group came after them in an attempt to stop them from leaving the country. *Meme* Ndateelela drove her car to find us at Ondjito village. While we were on our way we just heard the sound of a car behind us and then we started running but *Meme* Ndateelela brought along some men who were faster and caught us. After we failed to escape and run away *Meme* Ndateelela was preaching reminding us that we should stop the idea of leaving the country and we should go back to our homes.

I remember her pointing at me saying "Even you Simon as little as you are. Where do you think you are going? Do you want to die? You must go back home to assist your mother". She further shouted at me that "Go back home, who is going to fetch water for your mother?" At that time our village was facing water scarcity and there was nobody at home to help my step mother with household chores. After that she turned to her boys, "Elia and Festus you must go in the car right now." We agreed that we should go back home. I also jumped in their car with the boys.

While we were in the car going back we agreed that we would leave at midnight. Since the other three boys were from Oshali village and I was in Omundudu not far from each other, we agreed that I should be in Oshali village at their home around six in the evening. At six in the evening I took my suite case to join the other guys at Oshali. I went with my close friend and neighbor Kanduve. Around seven o'clock in the evening we met up with some of the guys at a bar of one of our relatives at Oshali. We started to ask ourselves whether our idea was still alive of leaving the country in the midnight. Everybody was excited and the plan was definitely on.

It was almost time for supper, my friend Kaduve went to the relative house and I went with the boys from *Tate* Shikukutu house. I remember sneaking in one of their rooms because my friends did not want me to be seen by their mother who had advised us to stop the idea of leaving for exile. Then one of my friends went to get their food prepared for supper and they called each other to eat at [1]*Olupale.* They ordered me to just stay in the room apparently they would make a plan for me. I was so hungry and thinking that those boys would eventually find the food delicious and forget to leave some for me. Finally they brought me some food in the plate and I enjoyed my food very much.

Then it was sleeping time, in fact it was taking a nap for few hours before we took our long walk to freedom. I think I had a nightmare seeing myself already carrying a gun in exile, come on don't blame me I was young and just excited. Our long walk into exile was a challenging one. The most challenge we faced was that we could not communicate in Portuguese which was the lingua franca of Angola by then. We could not ask questions about anything we wanted to know. We crossed the Namibia and Angola borders.

We first walked miles and miles in the midnight until we went into one house which belonged to an old man. We slept there until in the morning, we ate our porridge and moved on until we came to a town called Ondjiva, which was a pick up point. We were taken in a private car to the next town called Oshangongo. At Oshangongo we slept in a hostel type of facility. We spent two nights at Oshangongo. There was a river nearby where we were swimming. We were actually bathing in the river.

There were many groups of people big and small joining us at Oshangongo from Namibia. After two days the big truck came to pick us up. We were traveling throughout the night singing freedom songs. We were overjoyed and excited without having any idea of where we were going. Our next camp was Lubango. When we arrived at Lubango, we were strictly searched and screened. We were divided according to our ages, small children like us were told to go somewhere else while the grown-ups were in their own group. We came to

---

1   *Olupale* is an Oshiwambo traditional place where a man of the house and his boy children usually sit at a fire to eat and share men to men stories. It is also a first place where all visitors are welcomed and greeted.

learn that the older people were sent for training and we were waiting to be transported to another refugee camp. Many groups were coming in Lubango day after day and night after night. We were always excited to hear the sounds of big trucks and people singing when they were arriving at the parade. It was amazing, we used to go and see people who came from our villages and what news they brought from home. The arrival was always amazing. Indeed, those were breathtaking moments.

There was nothing to do for us children in Lubango since it was a transit Camp, we were only waiting for our next trip. However, there was a good soccer field and we used to play soccer there. I overstayed in Lubango for the next trip. After a second trip I went to ask from the office why my name was not included and the problem was sorted out. It was like first come first to go but I was left behind two times. The bad part was that every time there was a trip we were prepared with our luggage to go. I remember I had a broken suitcase and I used a rope around it to avoid my clothes falling off. It was fun! I was not impressed to keep on carrying my broken suitcase to the parade back and forth just because the secretary forgot to type my name in the list. If your name was not in the list you felt very disappointed. Also, it was not good to see people who just came after you leaving you behind.

Since I had been in the Camp for sometime, most officials asked me to volunteer at the office. My task was to go and call people who were in Lubango whenever there was a telephone call for them. I enjoyed running up and down calling people to go to the office for the telephone calls. Then the next trip came and my name was on top of the list. We went to Kwanza Sul refugee Camp. I remember it was my first time being in an airplane. We felt really honored. When we were informed about our flight we did not sleep out of anticipation and excitement thinking that we would be up there in the air. It was indeed a great feeling. Then the day came, we took our luggage and we were in the truck taken to the airport. It did not take us long to arrive in Kwanza and we were told to go in the big truck again that was prepared to transport us to the refugee camp. On our arrival at the camp we found a well-organized group of students to welcome us with freedom songs. Oh that was incredible, we were warmly welcomed in style.

Kwanza Sul Education Center

I could see that the center was way well developed. There was everything from the hospital, schools, dining hall, a big office and hostels. In terms of weather Kwanza was a cold place. Our first month of arrival it was very cold. Then we started attending classes to continue with my primary education. I was in Form IV and Ms. Kondja was our beautiful class teacher. I enjoyed my stay in Kwanza very much. The only challenge facing us was malaria of which most of my student friends were badly affected.

My best friends in Kwanza were Roberts and Neville. I vividly recall how we used to wake up early in the morning to go cook for others in the Center. We were put in different groups with the group leader to do different chores in the center on a rotational basis. Our group leader was Ms. Victoria, she was very tough on us. I enjoyed it when it was our group responsible for cooking and serving others. It was an amazing experience that I will forever cherish.

We always used to wake up earlier in the morning to do basic military exercises and physical activities. There were trenches as safe hiding places when there was an attack from the enemy. At times life was hard in the center. Luckily, I had two paternal relatives *Meekulu* Kakodi and my aunt. I visited *Meekulu* Kakodi many times at her house with her husband *Tatekulu* Kakodi. They were both very old. They had many fruit trees such as pawpaw and mangos that I used to enjoy eating very much. Most of my visits to *Meekulu* and *Tatekulu* Kakodi I brought along many pawpaw and mangos to the hostels to share with my friends too.

My aunt and her husband had a house near to our hostel. I visited her most of the time after she heard that there was a child of one of her relatives George. She was the one who left a message at the office that she needed to see me. She was the one who first took me to the Kakodi family and to my aunt Meme Aina who was a teacher at the center. Kwanza was special to me because I had many paternal family relatives who were taking good care of me and my basic needs.

One night I will never forget was when I went to have my delicious meal at her beautiful house. After the meal I had to take the left overs to the bin outside. There were a few long grasses, I just felt like I had stepped on a needle or something sharp. Oh, it was actually a snake bite on my right foot, it was terribly painful. Luckily my aunt was a nurse working at the hospital, she came to give me the first aid by cutting my foot and we could see dark and black blood. She was saying that was the poison and I was lucky. We did not find the snake that had bitten me. I was hospitalized for two weeks in Kwanza hospital. The snake bite came at a critical time because we were waiting to go on study missions. Kwanza was also a transit place before we went to another places. I was afraid to see others going while I was admitted in the hospital. My aunt who was a nurse at the hospital kept on reassuring me that I would not be left behind she would let me know if my name was in the list to go.

It was exactly two weeks before the list was displayed at the office for students to go for studying abroad and luckily for me it happened after I was discharged from the hospital. My name was in the list for students to go to Cuba and my friend Robert was in the list for Germany. My friend and I were happy going to study abroad even though we were not going to the same country. Robert and I never met again until today.

Study missions

Towards the end of the year 1988 most students studying at Kwanza were sent on study missions to different countries to continue with our education. Countries such as Cuba, East Germany (known by then as GDR), Bulgaria, Zambia, Congo Republic, Nigeria, Sierra Leone, Gambia and many other countries. My name was in the list of those who were going to Cuba. We were told to go to Luanda the capital city of Angola where we would finalize our Visa applications. I vividly remember our trip from Kwanza to Luanda in big and long TATA trucks. We were singing from the word go until our final destination Luanda. The spirit was quite high among us, children singing freedom songs with Jeep cars being driven up and down for communication to ensure that UNITA soldiers were not attacking us.

The road between Kwanza and Luanda was full of bushes, mountains and hills, it was very scary at times but God was with us until we arrived safely. When we arrived in Luanda we found our tents already erected and the Commissar was calling our names and ushered us to our temporary shelter. January 1989 Luanda Center was very busy with people coming in and going out. It was the time when the news came from Namibia that there would be elections and people were preparing to go back home. Most people of the voting ages were leaving the center to go and vote in Namibia. Most students who were abroad returned and they were also temporary accommodated at

Luanda Center. There were many flash news around and we were always alert to what was coming next.

One disappointing news we received was that all the students who were scheduled to leave for Cuba, the trip was cancelled due to elections in Namibia. On one hand we were happy that our country would gain its independence but on the other hand we were disappointed because we were no longer going to Cuba. After some weeks of waiting we were finally told that we were now going to African countries instead of going oversea. Some African countries were mentioned namely Nigeria, Congo, Liberia, Gambia and Sierra Leone. We had also our own wish list to make, for example my friends and I would say I wish my name will be in this or that country list. There was some rumors about special diet in Sierra Leone, oh that was funny and nearly all my friends were saying if that was the kind of food people eat there I am not going. In the end our names were displaced at the office and I was in the Nyango Education Center, Zambia list.

The day came to go to Zambia. We were informed that our passports were ready and we would be in the air once again from Luanda Airport to Zambian capital city, Lusaka. That was my second time in the airplane and the feelings were amazing. As usually we never suffered at the airport, there were always people to usher us where and what to do next. Our passports were usually collected from us and handed over to the counter while we were waiting for the verification and stamp. After the verification we were taken to the trucks that were parked outside to go to our final destination. The moment we got into our trucks the SWAPO spirit began of singing the freedom songs. It was a big convoy of cars and we were jubilating and singing on top of our voices heading to Nyango refugee camp. It took us a couples of hours before we arrived at the Nyango administration office. As usual other refugee girls and boys were already there waiting to welcome us.

Nyango Education Center

We arrived very late in the evening. It was a big place, we stayed in the hostels. I could say life in Nyango was totally different from all other places I stayed before. There were blocks of different classes, big hospital, a dining hall and two big hostels for both boys and girls. Life in Nyango Education Center was truly different, there was a weekly newsletter to keep us informed about current issues. Different entertainment groups were well established such as cultural troops, sport teams and musicians.

I mostly took part in Soccer and I was one of the youngest player with our coach Mr. Tjuku. We used to compete with big teams from Okaoma District. When there was a visiting team, the soccer field was usually full to capacity with those refugee boys and girls cheering up and down. Soccer was a very popular sport and we enjoyed it very much.

Another social event I used to enjoy in Nyango was known as Miss Nyango beauty pageant. The event used to attract a big crowd, good music and dancing competition. I still recall how we boys used to cross the river to go and attend the Miss Nyango event in the late evening. Girls' hostel was built far from the boys' hostel, so we were only allowed to go to the girls' hostel whenever there were events such as Miss Nyango Contest. It was true that my girlfriend took part in the event but she did not impress the judges. I was very proud to see her taking part.

When I think of how we were given humanitarian support like food, medicine and clothes by different nations of the world it humbles me to think how lucky we were at that difficult time. When it was time to get our clothes for example, we were usually told to go to the hall and there would be bundles of clothes. We were divided into different groups about ten of us making a circle and the bundle was at the center. The person in charge cut the bundle and clothes were spread all over for us to collect as many as we could. We did not care about the sizes, what was important we got enough clothes. That was our shopping moment to wear something new. It was living a refugee life but the good news was that we survived and our country was independent.

As refugee children, we also took our education very serious in Nyango Education Center. For example I enjoyed going to school every day. I did most of my school work exceptionally well. Everything about school was special. We had the best teachers, enough books and the teaching environment was supportive. I was particularly fascinated by the teaching of Mr. Shorter and Mbokoma. They were excellent teachers, inspirational and encouraging. I was even given an award for becoming the best third student in our class. It was a very special recognition of my hard work that has a special place in my heart forever. Generally, I loved being at school and reading my books.

I can summarize that as children who lived in SWAPO refugee camps, were never left to die from cold, hunger, diseases, illiteracy and thirst. Indeed we were given clothes to wear, food to eat, blankets and beds to sleep on, water to drink, medicine whenever we were sick and education that paved way to be where we are today. I salute and take my hat off to the support given to us as children during the liberation of our country Namibia.

When the news came that elections would be held in Namibia in 1989 and all people of voting ages should get ready to go and vote, I was in Nyango, Zambia. Unfortunately by that time I was 15 years old, I could not go back home to vote. Despite that we were kept abreast of the latest developments in our country and the excitement was unbelievable in the camp. I remember when the news reached us that SWAPO won the election and Namibia was free, we spent the whole day and night singing, dancing and celebrating. Oh, it was magical all over in the camp! Our faces were painted 'Freedom at last', likewise everyone and everywhere.

We were like soon or later we would go back home. Not after a long period when the news came from Namibia that our country was then independent and we should be repatriated to Namibia from November to December 1990. Nyango education center was a great place it was like home away from home and I enjoyed most of my adolescent time there. I never felt like I was in a refugee camp I think I had good friends who made me feel like we were the same family. I am trying to think the last thing I did before I left Nyango for Namibia but honestly I cannot remember what it was. I think I was too excited to go home.

Coming back to independent Namibia

When the repatriation process began I found myself boarding once again from Lusaka airport to Windhoek, Namibia. The airplane stopped in one country I cannot remember, all I can remember it took sometimes there while we were told to remain seated. I saw some people disembarking and some embarking. It is only now I am thinking that perhaps there was no direct flight from Lusaka to Windhoek by then. Anywhere after such a long wait we arrived safely at night in Windhoek. We spent a night at some place I did not know in Windhoek. The following morning I was in the big yellow bus going back home in the North. I came to learn that all other student returnees were accommodated at Mweshipandeka High school in Oshana region and that was where we were taken so that our families could come to finally take us home.

When we arrived at Mweshipandeka High School the SWAPO spirit was still higher and we started singing once again nonstop. It was a great reunion ever. It was a really nice to see nearly everybody there once again in an independent Namibia. The most exciting thing was reuniting with our friends from exile, some of them came earlier during election period and some of them came from different countries. I remember we started asking each other about our experiences from different countries we were staying. We spent a night singing and chatting. We laughed, joked and teased each other.

Since we came nearly at the beginning of school academic year, some of my friends and I were in the list to start our secondary education at Mweshipandeka High School. It was not long before my father spoilt the fun, he suggested that I should go home and attend the school that was closer to our home village. I had to leave Mweshipandeka and I went home to find if Eengendjo Secondary School had a space to accommodate me. That was how I left the school and my friends from exile. I was not really disappointed to leave for home, I think I was missing home too. I took my luggage and my single mattress and I got into a Taxi to the Oshakati Open Market.

I was lucky to find my uncle Mr. Werner who was excited to take me home. We first passed by his shop and he bought me a cool drink. It was ice cold and I jokingly asked if it was for me alone to drink. You should understand I was from the bush, a refugee boy. And it was time to get home. I remember my family was very excited to see me when I arrived home. Even neighbors came to welcome me. Those that were around to welcome me, they were asking me endless questions. I remember I had long hair, safe to say I was an Afro man. They were looking at me amazed. Some were touching my skin I could see they found it difficult to believe that I came back alive. It was an emotional moment considering that many Namibians did not come back home alive. As a Nation we lost many lives during the war of National liberation and freedom. It was good to see everyone that day too. I couldn't have been more happier to be back in the home I grew up in. I started walking around looking at every corner of the house and even the trees in the field. It really brought me beautiful memories.

Yeah and it was time to go sit in the house and start talking my life experiences in exile. Yho! My family was listening attentively as I was narrating my story. I even remember my step mother asked me how I sneaked out of the house and left her alone without telling her where I went. I just smiled and apologized to say that the aim was independence of our country. The following morning I never knew how the news spread that I was back in the country our dear family friends were coming in one by one to welcome me back. I kept on retelling my exile stories from one visitor to the next, same thing over and over. That kind of hospitality humbled me deeply considering that so many people cared about me and my wellbeing.

In the afternoon my childhood friend Kanduve with whom we could have gone together into exile if it were not for his cowardice and love of sleeping, we decided to walk around our beautiful village. By so doing we could meet my old friends and everybody. There were not much changes for the past three years I have been away from our lovely village. But honestly it was good to be back home and as the saying goes: the rest is history.

I came at the beginning of the school academic year and there was a need for me to find which school I would do my secondary education. After leaving Mweshipandeka High school the only choice I had was to go to Eengendjo Secondary School which was somewhat near to my home. Luckily to say the school principal was our closest neighbor and a family friend. Thus, my step mother advised me that I should go to his house to let him know that I needed to be at his school. When I went to see him, he first asked me to take a look at my school report. He then informed me that he could see I was doing a different education system and it was not easy for him to tell me exactly if I would be admitted. He only said I should go to the school so that they would see what to do. On the day we had agreed upon, I went to the school to see the principal.

MY SECONDARY EDUCATION

When I went to Eengendjo there were many other returnees also enrolling at the same time which was easy to manage than if I were the only one. We had a challenge about which grade to enroll in since we were using different education system in exile. The school authority decided to give us an aptitude test before we were finally admitted. They basically agreed that if one happened to fail the test he or she would be admitted in the grade lower than the grade we wanted to enroll in.

Fortunately enough, most of us passed the test very well. Our English was really good than most learners who were not in exile. During our years in exile, English was our day to day medium of communication and official language especially our group that was in Zambia. Studying at Eengendjo SSS was the nicest thing that ever happened to me. The school is situated in Omungwelume town in the Ohangwena region. The school and its surrounding was conducive for learning. Even our teachers were good to us.

Generally speaking, our teachers were learner-centered, friendly, hardworking and willing to assist us to pass very well. There was a healthy competition among all class teachers to have their learners perform at their best in all the subjects. Even though our school principal was the most feared person in the school, he wanted nothing from us learners other than to be the best we could be. He wanted us to focus in our education.

When the principal was around during our evening study the whole school observed a moment of silence. Every class was silent without any disturbance or noise from anywhere. Most of my teachers at Eengendjo were my favorites. On top of my best teachers were Mr. Bhinga for Agriculture subject and the late Mr. Wahengo for English subject. Mr. Wahengo was also my class teacher, he was the best man I could ask for as a teacher. He inspired and motivated us a lot. He used to talk at the general assembly as well and most learners enjoyed his motivational speeches. He spoke his heart out as a father talking to his children. I remember him when he was our class teacher warning my class mates that "Class, study hard and be careful that George boy, you will never catch him if you are playing." May his soul rest in peace.

During our time, many learners were working hard in their education. But there were few of the learners who were not doing very well. Mostly, the big boys who were in school for wrong reasons. They were either fighting others or stealing or going out to drink alcohol and coming back drunk. Especially on the weekends, it was not that safe and quiet all the time. The mature learners would go to drink during the day and come back to disturb everyone at night. They knocked at all the hostel rooms and when they felt like beating others, they would wake them up and slap them on the face.

I remember one day, my roommate was slapped by another man after going to the washrooms. They just called him, hei what are you doing out here (*paa!*) a slap on his face and he came in the room crying. We just started laughing. We were like: how come you were beaten just like that and you never fought back, boy.

There was one particular fearful man from the community who used to come to our school to beat everyone he met. One day he came in the school to disturb learners and the teachers who were on supervision duty informed the school principal. Our principal was well built, tall and strong and the community man was somehow shorter than him and slender. They were facing each other and wanted to fight, a fist fight.

The principal was saying I will cause damage to you boy, get out of my school and the boy was challenging the principal to a fight threatening to beat him in front of his learners. He first ran around and jumped on a nearby tree and dropped down like a monkey trying to intimidate the principal, all the time urging him to come and fight with him. The principal took the pistol out and the boy ran away.

We were all on our knees praying for a disaster not to strike. Those were some of the life experiences that we had. Other than that Eengendjo was a very beautiful school, a bit rural but I enjoyed my study time there. I mostly participated in sport especially soccer and volleyball. We did not win many soccer competitions when I was playing for our school soccer team but we won many volleyball tournaments. I was in most cases selected to play for the northern regional schools volleyball team.

I remember when my friend Abel and I were selected for northern schools regional team where we went to play in Windhoek. When we were there it was tough to make it for national volleyball selection. We met many tough teams and best volleyball players from Khomas region. We did not worry much about our poor performance in Windhoek we only enjoyed our trip to and back from the city. Abel and I had a good time in Windhoek.

On our way to Windhoek we looked so hungry until one of the soccer players better known by his soccer name as Fizi from Oshakati asked Abel and I that "Boys did you have something to eat?" I think he was tempted to ask us because whenever we had a stopover in a town for refreshments we were always left seated in the bus. If I can remember very well I think he gave us some money to go and buy something to eat.

Other players from well to do families used to jump out of the bus for shopping. When they were returning back in the bus they were carrying plastics full of food and drinks. For us the trip was a bonus we did not need to eat or drink anything we were fine but honestly we were not fine. We did not have money to buy whatever we wanted like others. Anyway, that is how life should be sometimes.

Back to education which is my passion, I can honestly say that I was a good learner and I left my name in the school's good books. I never failed a single grade and I was never asked to bring one of my parents at school due to misconduct. I was even elected to be a Learner Representative Council member responsible for Academic affairs in 1994 academic year. In general, my conduct as a learner was exemplary and encouraging. I remember I joined a group of few friends at school who were equally ambitious, the likes of Butty, Shipena, Eino and Freddy. We developed a good routine of waking up early in the morning to go to our classes in order to prepare for the day. We were always ahead of our classes, when other learners were coming we already had a privilege of studying before the school started.

My friend Butty was always number one throughout his school life so he was an inspiration to have as a friend. He worked and studied hard. His outstanding academic achievement was attributed to his hard work. We were in the same class just once in our lifetime, in grade 10 to be specific. As usual Butty took the number one spot in class and I was the second one. It was a tough and yet healthy competition we had in grade 10 in 1992. I remember Butty telling me that if I would like to be number one someday I should not be in the same class with him. I agreed to be in a different class because I knew he was truly brilliant and super intelligent.

The following year 1993 after we passed our grade 10 national examination I was in the same grade 11 with my friend Eino. Eino was equally the best learner. It was a tough competition in the class again. Our competition started from ordinary lesson class participation where I used to be vocal with a good command of English since I had just come from abroad and my friend Eino was somewhat limited in English vocabulary in terms of expressing the spoken language but brilliant mentally. I could also see that he was naturally well groomed, quiet and gifted. We first targeted the History test to see who would score high marks. It was a serious competition. We wrote the test and there we were waiting for the results. When our History teacher Mr. Kalomo brought the results, he too was aware of our competition. He made it clear that he wanted us to compete to get the best out of us. He announced his results from top to bottom. Eino and Gabriel were the first with 50/50 marks and I came second with 48/50.

It was a very bad day for me. Eino and Gabriel stood up shouting, yes, yes, we made it! It was true they made it but I did not like it when they were shouting and reminding us that they had done it while they knew I was the best. Of course I was not the best, I was just disappointed. After the teacher gave us our test back, I still remember I went after him complaining where he took my two marks. My argument with him was that after all it was just a History test with essays and all, it was easy for him to give me my two marks. There we were, reading my responses, saying here and there he was supposed to give me my two marks. When I came back to our class Eino and Gabriel started laughing and I started crying. I cried that day so loud and my friend Eino will never forget that day so easily. It was like I did not pick a better class because the class I picked Eino was the one taking the first number one spot. The following year 1994 I technically avoided to be with Eino and Butty in the same class.

I was in my own class where I ended up becoming number one, a position I have been fighting for since I came at Eengendjo SSS. Of course I loved education and to be the best was part of my education ambition. I therefore enjoyed my best moment knowing very well that I was the overall best man in class. I loved being a good boy doing my best at school.

Actually, I have been a good boy ever since my early school years, always focused and determined to achieve my educational goals. I think I can say I am a self-driven person. I was always a good child despite the fact that my parents were not there to watch over my steps and actions or not. This could partly be attributed to the fact that I grew up as an orphan boy without a mother and my father was always away at work, I ended up taking care of myself and in the process I became self-driven and independent.

I think I had different types of friends at school. But I can say that Butty, Shipena and Eino were my academic friends. I had some friends like Shali and Elia who were more like family friends giving each other social support. We supported each other socially, going out sometimes on Fridays to buy soft drinks and sweets. My friends Shali and Elia were from well to do families. They had always money to buy this and that at school. They used to invite me during school breaks to go buy fat cakes at the school main gate. We shared washing soaps, powders and Vaseline. At the time I had a fracture in my left leg from a soccer game at school in 1992, my friend Shali gave me his nice short trouser and some money when I was admitted in the hospital. He was there for me, taking me to the hospital and bought me some fruits on the same day that I was admitted. We were always there for each other, me, the poor boy and my friends, the rich boys. They saved my life in many big ways. I am forever grateful to them for their generosity and support.

I had also what I can call sport friends. My sport friends at Eengendjo were: Abel, Lukas, Lamek, Hosea and Tulonga. In most cases when there were sport events these were the type of friends I used to play with, watch sport and talk about sport. I can conclude by saying that I formed different type of friendships based on my interest and it was so unfortunate that I did not have the same common interests with most of the friends I had at Eengendjo. It simply means that I am a human being and unique.

As a human being sometimes I made my mistakes due to peer pressure or many other factors but in general I have no regrets as to how I conducted myself when I was at Eengendjo, considering that it was where I spent most of my adolescence years. In summary those were the highlights of my most memorable experiences when I was schooling at Eengendjo SSS in Omungwelume from 1991 to 1994.

MY FIRST JOB

This section takes the reader to my life journey as a man at the time I had finished my secondary education, moving a step further towards my first job in the factory in the town of Walvis Bay and then to Epundi Primary School as a grade one teacher. I was fortunate enough to have the year break of 1995 to put my early education at a test by finding a job.

Kohler Corrugated Company

I was first employed at Kohler Corrugated Company in Walvis Bay as a factory worker responsible for packing boxes to be delivered to different companies. The job was very interesting since I was working in the same company with my father. We used to work in different shifts namely morning shift from 6:00 AM to 6:00 PM and evening shift from 6:00 PM to 6:00 AM.

In most cases my father and I were not in the same shifts, I thought he made such arrangement so that there would always be someone at home. At times I wished we were in the same shift especially one day when I almost had a fight with a co-worker. He was ever challenging me as why I only spoke English and not Afrikaans language. The majority of the employees in the factory did not know English, they were only speaking Afrikaans because they did not really get formal education. I was angry because he sounded more like a racist and a bully. Another reality was that my Afrikaans was not good at all even if I wanted to speak it, it was difficult. I remember crying so hard in the changing room until my father came to ask me what had happened. Most employees were shocked looking at a young man crying and they wanted to know what exactly happened. We were called in the office by our supervisor and he warned us not to disturb each other anymore.

In spite of that incident I enjoyed my first job very much especially the pay day. We were paid every end of the week roughly N$2000-00 and sometimes with overtime we could get N$3000-00. It was good money. In fact it was where my love of shopping started. I spent my money on food, shoes and clothes. My best friends at work were: Werner, Samuel and Tate Henok. As my father was well known in the company I was given sort of special treatment by nearly all co-workers. Many a times whenever I walked within the company I could hear co-workers telling each other that I was George's child and things like that.

I took a two weeks leave in May to visit my home village. Since I started my job I never went back home to visit my family and friends. Arriving home everybody was happy to see me. I was telling my family about my new job and how rewarding it was. When I arrived home I was informed that there was a schools sport's tournament at Oshimwaku a nearby village. I did not hesitate I went the following day on Saturday morning to go and watch some games. As I was a sport fan, the tournament was really good and well attended. I also met many people there.

Among the people that I met was *Tate* Werner my uncle, he was very excited to see me. He started asking where I have been and if I was working somewhere. I told him the truth that I was with my father working in the same company in Walvis Bay. He then said he had a job offer for me to become a teacher at Shituwa Secondary school. He was the Principal of the school by then. He asked me if I was still interested so that I could take my certified copies to his house on Monday morning before he left for work. I was fascinated by such urgent news, I did not waste any time I left the tournament immediately for home. I got my grade 12 certificate and my Identity document then I went to Omungwelume to make copies and get them certified.

I did not sleep enough on Sunday night because of a fear that I might be late to take my copies in the morning as we agreed with my uncle. Around 5:15 AM I was already up washing my face ready to take my copies. I arrived at my uncle's house on time, he was still getting ready for work. He came to me and I gave him my copies. He quickly browsed through and said everything was well in order and he would come back to me in two or three weeks' time. I thanked him for his care and support and I went back home.

By then I faced a dilemma of not knowing the best choice I should make after the two weeks. I had not make up my mind as yet as to whether I should go back to my job in Walvis Bay or wait to start my new job as a teacher. I was well aware that my leave would be up in the next week and I felt that it would be difficult to go and come back again. I did not know how I came to the conclusion to finally decide that I would not go back to my job in Walvis Bay anymore. I stayed until I got the final response from my uncle.

It was exactly after two weeks I went back to consult my uncle on the job offer as he had promised. When I went to his house he politely told me that his school board agreed to take a different person who had applied before me and that she had some teaching experience compared to me. He then shared with me that I needed not to worry because he already spoke to his wife *Meme* Rauna to appoint me at her school as a teacher.

Meme Rauna was a school principal at Epundi Junior Primary school. In just few days *Meme* Rauna invited me to come sign some forms of appointment and that she was expecting me to start on the 1st June 1995. Then I went to start my new job as a teacher at Epundi Junior Primary School.

Epudi Primary School

Before I knew it I was welcomed at Epundi Primary School, a school that opened the doors for me to make a better world for myself. I was given to teach grade 1 in the same class with my life time mentor *Meme* Paarti. She taught me many things especially how to work with children. My main tasks were to collect homework books, distribute books to children and take them to Physical Education period outside to play.

The first three months I was mainly assisting my mentor to keep the order in the class. The last three months I was then delegated to mark the homework books and to teach reading and writing. We used to take the children outside to write on the sand different words. I used to walk from one child to another to see how they wrote their words. I learned to respect my grade one teacher because teaching Grade one it was not easy to develop such skills of reading and writing. As a teacher you must be patient enough to overcome the challenges of teaching small children how to read and write.

On many occasions I used to teach English at grade 6 and it was really good to work with somehow big students than grade one. Many grade 6 students were happy to see me in their class and help me with speaking English. I also used to teach English in grade 5, on the invitation of an English teacher Ms.

Paulina. She used to say "Simon please come help my students with English today". The English lessons in grade 5 and 6 used to help me not to forget how to speak English as well.

When I was at Epundi I was young and passionate about sport, especially soccer. During my leisure time I was a soccer player coach for our school team. I should admit that we had small boys and they were too young to compete with many schools. Notwithstanding, I organized my small boys and wrote a letter to challenge Omundudu Combined School in a game of soccer. I thought Omundudu would turn down our invitation to play with them but to my surprise they responded positively. Omundudu was really the best and they had big and good soccer players.

The date came and we went to their school. It was a memorable match which many of us would never forget. I was playing as a defender and I was truly technically blocking their strikers to score. The moment the ball was kicked in front I ran away for an offside. The strikers couldn't move. My initial tactic was to frustrate the strikers to commit many off sides to such extent that they would give up running for the ball. The game ended in 1-1 all draw. We were the first to score and they had to score in the last minutes of second half. It was tough and technical. I could see that the boys were happy to draw with a school like Omundudu. Since the game was played on Friday, the following week on Monday the school principal asked me to tell everybody how the game went. When I announced the good news that we drew with Omundudu Combined School, everybody at the assembly was applauding and clapping for the boys. I got the feeling that we had somewhat made history for our school.

Epundi was a good place to work. There were wonderful colleagues I remember *Meme*: Rauna, Victoria, Paulina, late Paarti and Beatha and the late *Tate* Justus Uomu. By then the school had more female teachers and only the two of us were male teachers. We were privileged enough because our female colleagues reassured us that the male teachers needed not to come with lunch boxes, they would take care of us and they did that very well. They were really good-hearted people. Since I was appointed as a temporary teacher I left Epundi Primary School after my contract in December 1995.

Windhoek International School

When my contract ended as a temporary teacher at Epundi Primary School, the following year 1996 I was admitted to study at the University of Namibia (UNAM) in Windhoek. As a poor orphan boy studying away from my home village without any reliable family financial support it was very difficult for me to cope during my studies at UNAM. There were many hard times where I did not have even a single penny to buy a fat cake to eat. I remember at one point my body soaps and lotion were finished and I did not know where to get the money to buy them.

It was really difficult without groceries and other basic necessities. I just used to lock myself inside my room to cry out and pray. On the other hand I decided to stay focused on my studies and kept a distance from many people to avoid being misled. It was then that I developed the love for watching television, there were many television programs I used to watch, my number one favorite being the Seventh Heaven and Moesa programs. I also enjoyed other programs such as Generations, Friends, Mr. Cooper and The Shadow.

Even though I was a temporary teacher the previous year before I went to study, the little money I saved was finished due to transport from the north to Windhoek. God is truly amazing, I did not know how it came about perhaps God saw my situation to open a door for me at Windhoek International School. Since one of my majors was sport science I was informed by one of my Human Movement Lecturers that there was a gentleman from a local school looking for a coach and that she gave my name. She gave me the telephone number to call in order to confirm my interest.

It was a great opportunity for me at least to be able to cope from my hardship when I became a coach of boys under 12 years at Windhoek International School, better known as WIS. It was a great honor to serve in the international community. My appointment was not merely about getting money I was very committed and working hard. I should also add to say that I have been a sport fan all my life.

I also love working with children, they just make me happy to see them happy. As a school, we played many games with other schools around Windhoek and we won most of our games. I remember that soccer team very well, with their captain Andrew from England. Andrew was a very good young soccer player with his dribbling skills, he was a joy to watch. I will not be surprised if I see him in Manchester United lineup one day or best playing for England soccer team.

Honestly speaking, WIS completely changed my financial situation, at least I could then buy my groceries and other basic supplies. The school was paying me good money enough for a student to survive. It was from some of that generosity I learned to believe that God is truly watching and taking care of us. I had been coaching WIS from 1997 and I left in 1999 after I had completed my studies at UNAM. If it were not for the long distance from where I was employed as a teacher I could have been still serving the school for as long as I could. However, I would like to thank Windhoek International School for its support as part of social responsibility to contribute to my welfare. If it were not for the support given I could have either dropped out of university or my studies could have been negatively affected in one way or the other. I thank WIS for the support and I would like to say it should continue supporting needy and poor students like me, its support changed my life for the better and WIS can still change many more poor students' lives.

MY TERTIARY EDUCATION

In this section I write about my first tertiary education journey at the University of Namibia as a poor village boy studying in Windhoek Capital City. I also write my experiences when I was studying at the University of Fort Hare in South Africa.

Applying for admission

Toward the end of 1995 I applied for admission to further my studies at the University of Namibia. At the time of my application I was a temporary teacher at Epundi Primary School and it was for that reason I applied to become a teacher. I made many attempts to further my education at many institutions including Ongwediva College of Education where I was shortlisted and interviewed for admission. I was not alone when I was applying for admission, I was with my best friend Joseph Nangombe. By then we were staying with our relatives in Oshakati in close neighborhood. We were sharing ideas and advised each other where to apply and how to fill in our application forms.

We first went to Ongwediva College of Education for our interviews. Luckily Joseph was admitted after the interview and I was put in the waiting list. I remember when Joseph was counseling me that I should not worry there would eventually be a place to join him at the College. We were truly supporting each other. It was just in a few days after the interview outcome, we received confirmation letters of admission from UNAM.

Joseph and I knew that even if we were admitted at UNAM it would not be possible for us to go without a bursary since our parents would not afford to pay for our education. I shared my lack of financial support to one of my friend I met at Secondary School who was already at UNAM by then. He gave me an office telephone number that I should call to inquire about my bursary application. I did call the office as I was advised by my friend but the office said that they were still busy allocating bursaries to lucky students. After some few weeks I had even lost hope to study at UNAM and then one of my friends Butty called informing me that the list of bursary was out and my name was on the list. I was so happy. In fact it was not only my name even the name of my best friend Joseph was there as well. It was our time and there was nothing to stop us anymore to go and study.

The day finally came, we found ourselves in the bus going to Windhoek. To be honest we did not know for sure where we were going to spend the night following our registration day. We were just happy to be on our way and God would take care of the rest. We arrived very well at night in Windhoek. The bus dropped us at Soweto market where I asked people to direct us to the house of uncle Shimwafeni. God was truly with us, we never found it difficult to find my uncle's house. We spent our night there and woke up early in the morning to go to UNAM for registration.

Studying at the University of Namibia

When the Taxi dropped my friend Kassy and I at the UNAM main gate we suddenly became very excited. I remember telling my friend that: my brother here we are and we are now university students. He joked by saying hei Simon George just hold on and do not start rejoicing as yet until we are officially registered as students. He warmed me that this is just still a dream we still need to find the registration hall and take it from there. I looked at him not convinced because I knew deep down in my heart that everything would go according to the plan. I just said let us keep moving forward my brother, we have a registration hall to look for and get ourselves registered.

We were moving and moving really fast, aimlessly and carelessly looking at big UNAM buildings and city life all over the place. You know to us village boys anything and everything in the city looked so fancy and breathtaking. We asked a group of students to show us where the registration hall was and how to get there. In less than two minutes time we found ourselves in the hall queuing up. We were first in the wrong queue until we heard other students asking about which queue is for education students. Kassy whispered that we should go to the correct queue.

First of all we were at a verification desk, where the officials were looking at our certificates, subjects, counting points and perhaps looking at many other things. Kassy was in front of me therefore his documents were the first to be verified. I saw him given a go ahead to the next desk. Then it was my turn, the official looked at my face like I did something wrong and she asked who I was and where I came from. I almost asked if all people were first asked their names and where they came from or it was a special treatment for me as a poor village boy. I never challenged her but I was honest to say my name is Simon George and I am from Omundudu village. After I answered her questions, she showed little interest to my response.

I still have this concern why people ask things and then they are not interested in the answers. She made me feel like why did she ask me so many questions and then paying little interest when I answered her. After she did her verification by looking in my certificate and putting my points together she then showed me the next desk to go. Excitement was still farfetched, I was just biting my nails let this process be over and be declared as a university student already. I was internalizing and praying deep in my soul that let everything go well in this hall, God help me. At my next desk I was asked to choose my major subjects that I would like to specialize at the university.

I first did not know what to choose I then went to ask my friend Kassy what his major subjects were so that I could build on that. I found that he had chosen History, his favorite subject and Physical Education. He asked me to look into my certificate the subject I had a better grade in and he advised me that I should think along those lines. Looking at my certificate I scored very well in Business Economics and Biology. I therefore chose to specialize in Economics and Physical Education.

Even though I faced some challenges here and there my first degree studies at the UNAM were a marvelous experience. I did not encounter problems of not attending my classes or failing my modules. I really did exceptionally well as far as academic work was concerned.

Nearly all my subjects were important to my personal and professional development and growth. For example I enjoyed my major subjects especially from economics the following modules were quite interesting and I passed them very well too: Principles of Economics, Micro Economics, Monetary Economics and Foundations. I think I was more so interested in the way the lecturers of these modules were giving their lectures. They were very professional and I can still remember Selma and Omu with their sense of humor, they were the best Economics lecturers.

When it came to Physical Education major, there were many modules I loved and passed exceptionally well. For example, Leisure and Sport, Psychological and Sociological Aspects of Sport, Indoor Ball Games and Raquet Sport modules. Generally, education modules were also fascinating, for example, I loved Special Education, Counseling and Guidance, Sociology of Education and Teaching Practice.

Talking of Teaching Practice, I did my first School Observation and Teaching Practice at Oshakati Senior Secondary School in 1997 and 1999 respectively. I still have those wonderful memories of my Teaching Practice at Oshakati SSS. I had subjects such as, Economics, Business Studies and Physical Education. I loved teaching so much. I remember more than one occasion when students from different classes used to stand at my class door watching me teaching. I could hear them saying "excuse me let me see him." I had a good time doing my Teaching Practice. I scored an A-grade in Teaching Practice, I was the best student teacher. During my Teaching Practice at Oshakati I was with my best friend Kassy, Laila, late Sam and Abed.

Coming back to my studies, I spent most of my leisure time at UNAM reading my novel books at the Language Center, surfing internet at the library and watching TV. I spent most of my time playing sport such as Soccer and Squash as well. I played for Tough Guys Football Club and UNAM Rangers Football Club respectively. Tough Guys Club was dominated mainly by Herero origin students studying at Namibia University of Science and Technology. We were only two players who were Oshiwambo-speaking. It was the best ever club in the UNAM domestic League. In my last two years of study I moved to UNAM Rangers F.C. It was a new team formed mainly by students from the Coastal part of Namibia and it was the best team. When we first started the Club we won the Domestic League with a great margin of points. I was a middle field player. My two best friends at the time I was studying towards BEd course were Ronny and Richard. I completed my four years Bachelor of Education degree in 1999 and graduated in April 2000 at Safari Hotel.

After one year of teaching I was interested to study further the following year. I therefore enrolled for a Specialized Post-Graduate Diploma in Special Education in 2002. The course was offered by UNAM on the distance mode. I learned quite a lot about different types of disabilities namely: Specific Learning

Difficulties; Hearing Impairment, Disability and Handicap; Intellectual Impairment, Disability and Handicap; Emotional Behavior Difficulties and General Special Needs Education. I specialized in Emotional and Behavior Difficulties.

The course was conducted via video-conferencing facility from UNAM main campus to Oshakati Campus where I used to attend my lectures every late afternoon. I would say studying on part-time was somewhat a challenge for instance the distance from the work place to the lecture venue was a bit problematic. As a group we usually had a problem to meet our group assignment deadlines because we were all working at different regions and places far away from each other. Those were the kind of challenges that we faced. If I can remember very well as a cohort we were not that a big group, I think we were around ten students. Some of my class mates were: Vistorian, Simon, Sorty, Selma, Tangeni, Abed and some names I cannot remember now like the big man who was a school principal and few others.

I did my Teaching Practice for Special Education course at Gabriel Taapopi Senior Secondary School in Oshana Region. The Teaching Practice went very well. I selected the school because it was an inclusive school admitting some learners with visual and hearing disabilities.

The course was definitely an eye opener for me. It really provoked my career interest in the fields of Special Education and Educational Psychology in general. The course assignments made it much easier to relate what I was learning in the class and see how I could use it in my practice as a teacher. For me the course helped me to even understand the learners' abilities and disabilities and the best practical methods to use for the benefit of all my learners. I did a mini-dissertation focusing on the contributing factors toward school drop-out of orphan children as a case study. It was actually where my interest of studying about orphan children's psychosocial support which I went to do at PhD level developed. I completed the course successfully and graduated in April 2004.

Studying at the University of Fort Hare, South Africa

Towards the end of 2007 academic year I applied to do a Master's Degree in education at the University of Fort Hare in South Africa. Two weeks after I sent my application, I received an email of acknowledgement. It did not take me long before I received another email from the university inviting me for a screening interview.

First of I was asked to write my statement of intent and that I would need to present it face to face to the committee of which the decision would be taken based on my presentation. I wrote my research intent accordingly and sent it before the due date. I had one big challenge to overcome, that was to go to South Africa and find East London. I made several calls to the university administrator enquiring about how to get there. She was very patient, friendly and encouraging. She provided me with the best alternatives how to get to East London and at University of Fort Hare.

In the end I booked the Inter cape bus from Windhoek to Cape Town and then the following day I managed to take another Inter cape bus from Cape Town to East London. It took me one night to arrive in East London. When I arrived at the bus station I asked the cab to take me to the campus. I was dropped at the campus within a short period of time until I found myself seated waiting to be called in for an interview.

A few weeks later I got an email informing me that I was admitted in the program. February 2008 was the time I was admitted to do my Master of Education (MEd) degree with the University of Fort Hare at the main campus in Alice. I was very excited to be admitted. My program supervisor was Prof Rembe. She was an angel, warm, friendly, understanding and supportive. She knew how to handle her students in order to complete on the record time period. I graduated in 2010 two years after my enrolment.

Before I completed my MEd, my eye was ever on doing my PhD. I did not even wait to graduate in order to apply for admission to the program. I applied without my MEd degree but some faculty members felt that I should have waited after the graduation in May in order to apply. I can honestly say that I was fortunate enough to be invited to the screening interview. I followed the same admission criteria and procedure of writing my research intent and then I went to present it to the committee.

During the interview the Dean of Faculty of Education was reminding me that I was lucky to be allowed to go through the admission process even before I graduated with my MEd. The graduation was scheduled to be held in May 2010 and I applied already in November 2009. Since my results were already available they decided to allow me to go through the admission process.

During the presentation there were many tough questions from the Panel members. Interview results came out after some weeks and I was admitted. It was really tough to have gone through the admission process. There was one particular staff member Dr. Brown who was a brilliant scholar and he was the most feared staff member by most postgraduate students. He knew research very well and he was truly gifted and highly intelligent. In the process Dr. Brown and I became good friends. I learned a lot from him. When I was writing my proposal I would send him my work for advice and support especially on the methodology part.

PhD was not a walk in the park, it was a tough program. I should say that being with the university from my Master's program it helped me in understanding what was expected of me to do my work within the shortest possible time. It was within six months of registration that my proposal was already in the hands of Research and Higher Degrees Committee. My PhD research was in the Educational Psychology field titled as: *A phenomenological study of orphaned learners' experiences with regard to psychosocial support provisioning in Namibia.*

I had two months of data collection in Namibia particularly in Endola circuit in the area of my birth. What I used to do in order to speed up the process I combined data collection with data analysis. I was collecting data during the day and in the evening I would do data analysis. I used phenomenological research design of which it was only fair I analyzed data while I could still remember the lived experiences of the participants. After my follow ups to clarify or confirm certain things with the participants I was reliably informed by most school principals that most orphans who took part in the research were somehow seen changed in the positive way. I was informed that they were more committed to attend school regularly and eagerly shown interest to work hard in school.

During my PhD studies I met many good people who helped me to get things done on time, especially from the Ministry of Education in Namibia, Ohangwena Regional office, Endola Circuit and school principals. I truly cannot thank them enough. I had the best supervisor ever. Luckily she started with me at Master's program, so we knew each other very well. I remember in the beginning we had our shortcomings here and there but I am just happy that in the end she nurtured me and given me her undivided attention to complete my studies on a colorful record period. I should also thank my supervisor for the Supervisor-link Scholarship I was awarded through Govan Mbeki Research and Development Center for my entire studies.

WORK AND CAREER

I already talked about the first year I started working which was a short period of just one year after completing my secondary education. This section provides insight of my professional life starting from my humble beginning working at Oshimwaku Combined School, Iipumbu SSS, Ongwediva Teachers' Training College, University of Namibia and University of Fort Hare.

Oshimwaku Combined School

The year was 2000 when I started my work and career as a teacher at Oshimwaku Combined School. The school is in Ohangwena Region and in the Endola Circuit in particular. Simply put, the school is in the region of my birth and closer to my home village. My career ambition was to start from home so that I would be able to support my family. I was initially placed in Karas Region down in the Southern part of Namibia but by that time my father was ill so I felt I should be working at the school much closer to home in order to take care of him. It was then that I applied to work at Oshimwaku Combined School.

My father was very excited about my idea to work from home. January 2000 was a good month after the school reopened, we were introduced as new teachers with my best friend and colleague Gerhard Iipumbu. We were very enthusiastic about starting our career in the rural school. I would say the school lacked basic resources such as conducive classrooms and teaching materials. We were also not happy about the school's poor performance which was due to poor motivation among students.

Our first three months were characterized by observing and getting to understand the school cultural norms and values. We spent most of our time sharing ideas on what we should do as young new teachers to bring about the desired results. I used to talk many times during our morning devotion about the importance of learning and that learners should take their education very serious.

My time as a teacher at Oshimwaku was well spent. It was really worth it. We brought about many changes at the school, some of our initiatives included awarding our best learners, learner-mentor support and grade 10 special motivation sessions. More and more of our learners started to work hard in their education. We started sharing the school vision in terms of where we wanted the school to be in the circuit ranking. Our learners' performance was number one priority.

We also reshuffled teachers by strategically allocating subjects in line with their qualifications and experiences. I for example was given to start English at grade 5 to 7. Meanwhile my friend Gerry who was a language specialist took over from grade 8 to 10. Our idea was that learners needed a strong language foundation and to be passed over in the hands of language expert who would help them acquire more advanced competencies. I remember how I started organizing open school drama day. We invited everyone from the teachers, principal, parents and other learners to come and witness how small boys and girls from grade 5 and 6 were speaking English. My learners enjoyed those moments.

I was also given Business Management subject to teach from grade 8 to 10. From the non-promotion subject I was given Physical Education and Life Skills from grade 8 to 10. We were also doing very well in sport. I was responsible for Netball as a coach and my friend Gerry was our soccer coach. Gerry was a very skillful soccer player. We both used to play with our learners in a school soccer team. Whenever there was a sport tournament, we were the most feared team especially if Gerry and I were on the field playing.

My best game with our school soccer team took place at Ehafo school tournament. Our school was playing Onepandaulo Combined School. It was a tough match and I really felt, we played exceptionally well. Learners used to sing our names and cheered us on, it was an incredible feeling. The match ended in a 2-2 goals draw, but our school was fortunate to win in the penalties.

One thing I would not forget what we did at Oshimwaku was the fact that we used to organize our soccer boys to work in the community as well. It was an initiative we came up with to generate some income for our sport development and to supplement the school sport budget. Most parents and community members used to ask for our soccer boys to work in their *Omahangu* field and paid them some money. We had three days in a week for community work usually after school working hours.

It was a good initiative working with the boys out there in the community. Some of the community members were too old to work in their fields so they solely depended on my boys to help them. We were admired and appreciated by many people in and around the school community. Sometimes parents came personally at the school to ask for the support, sometimes they wrote letters which were written in an old fashioned style and some simply sent people by word of mouth if we could go help them with their fieldwork.

As teachers after the school knocked off we usually kept ourselves busy coaching our school teams in the afternoon until evening. After the training I had to plan for my lessons for the following day and sometimes take time off to read my books. There were also many days where my friends and colleagues Neema, John, Gerry and I spent some quality time playing snooker and shared some drinks at the local shops near the school.

I had an incredible time at Oshimwaku. However, there were some challenges especially during the rainy season. There were two main oshanas that I had to cross before I got to school. It was really tough always crossing deep waters in the cold morning from one oshana which was next to our house and the other oshana near the school. I always took a short trouser and my formal long trouser that I had to change after crossing the deep waters. I was ever afraid of snake bites but I can say God saved me to cross the two big oshanas without anything bad happening to me.

When my father died in June 2000 it was even more difficult. After his passing on I bought my house beginning of 2001 in the Ongwediva town about 40 Kilometers away from the school. During the rainy season it was really difficult to reach the school on time especially since I was hiking from Ongwediva, my new home town. I therefore saved enough money and I bought my second hand car in 2002 which made things somehow better. Truly speaking I enjoyed driving to and from the school.

Another challenge by then was with regard to teachers' accommodation. Even though as a school we turned one classroom into two teachers' rooms to accommodate some of the teachers who came from far away regions. We were calling it "*Oshingolo* house" I never knew why we gave the house such a name. There was a serious need of teachers' accommodation but I was reliably informed recently that the problem was long solved.

Of course there is no doubt or whatsoever I loved Oshimwaku with all my heart. I never worked so hard in my teaching career than what I did at Oshimwaku Combined School, it was really a special school and I will always treasure this memory of myself teaching there. Upon our arrival at the school as new teachers, the school did not have proper school fence and the budget was not well recorded and accounted for. Things were not just done strategically with proper planning. We decided that there was a need to turn things around at Oshimwaku.

We first started meetings after meetings to draw up the budget and priority list. School development fund was well paid but never accounted for and nobody challenged the lack of accountability. We started changing people who were responsible for school finance and budgeting. To cut a long story short, we successfully erected the school fence in 2002, we managed to write a proposal for administration block and it was approved, built and handed over to our school in 2003. I remember after the completion of our administration block it was a big happy moment for the school community. We were there given our new offices by the school principal. Our principal was very happy that day too. He said to me with a big smile "*Tate* George you see our school is now beautiful." He was a very proud man. It is pity that he is no longer with us, to read this book. He was proud of me and treated me with respect, he was ever calling me "*Tate* George how can we do this and that let us talk about it." I miss him, may his soul rest in peace.

In addition to changes we brought at the school, I remember classes were very dirty and messy. Our early observation was that learners did not feel proud of their school. For example there was an old block where classes had some holes more like little doors. Sometimes while I was in the middle of my teaching, small learners just ran through the hole in the class and passed through it back again. It was very bad and chaotic. We decided in the meeting that all classes that had small holes should be attended to as a matter of urgency. Every class teacher was tasked to seriously ensure that the class was cleaned every day in the morning before the first period.

There was a specific committee that was chaired by *Tate* Lukas who was responsible for cleanliness and hygiene at the school. Within the classrooms and school surroundings things were thrown everywhere from papers, plastics and tins. The committee, with the support of class teachers and learners did amazing work. The school started to adopt a new healthy culture. There was really great change and even learners themselves could see that as teachers we meant business. All these changes effected at the school translated into improvement in the learners' achievement and performance. Learners' performance particularly grade 10 improved by a big margin and the circuit started to take our school more serious.

We were really pushing for a change. Even though my colleagues and I were working hard to bring about improvement at a school I knew very well that Oshimwaku was not my permanent place of work. I would move one day but I did not know when and how. I left Oshimwaku Comb. School in 2003 transferring to Iipumbu Senior Secondary School.

Iipumbu Senior Seconday School

My transfer as an ordinary teacher from Oshimwaku Combined School to Iipumbu Senior Secondary School brought some relief in my life. I needed a change but I never knew how and when the change would happen. At that time I was on study leave doing my teaching practice at Gabriel Taapopi Secondary School for my Special Education Postgraduate study. When the news came from one of my best childhood friend Butty who was teaching at Iipumbu at a time, that they had a vacant post and they urgently needed a teacher who specialized in Commerce. He advised me that if I was interested I should apply as quickly as possible.

I remember that in fact I applied desperately the same night I got the news. There was one big challenge I needed to face. It was to convince my school principal to sign my transfer form. Oh, that was a mind spinning game! I was contemplating throughout the night what I would say and how to say it. The news came on Friday afternoon and I planned to drive early on Saturday morning to get my transfer form and get it signed.

Saturday morning came and my friend Eino and I were on the road driving to Oshimwaku village to the house of my school principal. It was too early in the morning. We really never talked much about what I would say to ask for the transfer but I had a white lie in my mind. Forgive me God I lied to my principal but I was too desperate to move on with my career. Before we knew we were at my principal's home.

First it was a young lady who came to us and we did some cultural rituals of sitting down and politely greeting each other before we asked to see the principal. Before I got the response my heart kept on pounding, please let the principal be home and in a good mood. Then she said *Tate* was home and she asked us whether it was for good news since we had come too early. We quickly responded that it was a good news. Then the principal came to us and asked how he could help us so early in the morning.

I first reminded him that my teaching practice for the program I was doing was going very well and I was assessed where I scored good marks. Then I lied that the Lecturers who came to assess my teaching practice recommended me to do the Master of Education program the following year at Windhoek main campus. Since they were still around they asked me if they could go with my transfer forms already signed to Windhoek so that they could find a temporary school to teach to support me while I was studying.

My principal then asked me: "Tate George how long is your study leave?" I responded enthusiastically that it would take me only two years and I would come back straight to Oshimwaku Combined School. I then handed him the forms to sign. But I was afraid, to tell the truth. He just said it was fine with him and told me to take the forms to *Tate* Aron, the Head of Cluster.

Tate Aron was a tough man. He was one of our close neighbors at the village and we did not like each other that much. I was afraid to face him and afraid for his rejection at the same time. I told my friend Eino that we should go to see the man and I was not sure what the outcome would be. So we went to his house.

It was his wife *Meme* Ndamona who came to first greet us. *Meme* Ndamona and I were good friends, she was like a mother to me. We told her that we had come to see and talk to *Tate* Aron, her husband. She went to call him and he came to see us. I was straight to the point. I informed him that there was a study opportunity for me the following year and I brought my transfer forms for his signature. I was literally shivering of the big man as I was handing him the forms to sign.

Meanwhile he was receiving the forms, he posed a tough question: "Simon if you are going for study the following year, why did you need the transfer forms signed for?" I was still shivering of course avoiding eye contact, I responded that I would need to find a school to work and study at the same time. And he further asked "How long are you going to be away for your study?" I said only two years and I would come back straight to my school. He kept on asking whether we had agreed with my principal before he signed. We collectively said the principal was happy before he signed the forms. He then signed and said we must take the forms to the Circuit Inspector for her signature. There were so many people to see and sign the forms.

Our next stop was Endola Circuit Office, it was on Saturday still in the morning, the Circuit Office was opened. We first had our doubts if the Circuit office would be opened on Saturdays. I first went through the Secretary and asked to talk to the Inspector. Luckily the Circuit Inspector was in the office working. I went in her office after she had invited me. I told her the same thing of studying the following year and that I would need a school to work while I was studying to support myself. She asked me to write a letter clearly stating what I would do, where and for how long. It was somehow difficult to lie in writing but I managed to write what she asked of me. After that I could see she was busy, she just asked her Secretary to make copies of my forms and we left. I took my application and transfer forms to my friend Butty who took them to their school. It was after few days I received a call that I must report urgently at Iipumbu SSS to go start working there.

After one week or two there were news that my former principal was angry because of my transfer to Iipumbu SSS and not for the study as I had told him. He phoned the school Principal and even the Director so that I could return to Oshimwaku. The school principal of Iipumbu was saying that there was a vacancy and George had applied and the School Board found that I had met the requirements. The school decided that it was not ready to send me back. It was a big thing. My principal and I even spoke to Endola Circuit Inspector on the phone asking me to go back and why I had lied to them. I remember my friend Eino as well saying that I was lucky I could have lost my job for good. I continued teaching at Iipumbu because my transfer was already signed and approved by all relevant offices including the Director of Education.

When I transferred to Iipumbu SSS I was teaching Business Management at grade 10 and Business Studies at Grade 11. The following year in 2004 I was teaching Business Studies at Grade 12. I had some of the best students in Business Studies from Grade 11 and 12 respectively. I remember some of my best Business Studies students like Saara, Anna, Amon, Tangeni, Victoria and Brown. At Iipumbu I was also teaching Life Skills and Physical Education as non-promotional subjects.

I participated in some committees such as Sport Committee, Disciplinary Committee and Entertainment and Beautification Committee. I vividly recall when we organized Miss Iipumbu 2003 event which was the most outstanding event of the year. We generated a lot of money through selling of tickets. We bought a Television Set and Sound system for the school with the money we had generated. I was also a Netball coach when I was at Iipumbu. My Netball team was very tough. Some of my colleagues and friends at Iipumbu were: Butty, Joel, Denis, Natalia, Justy, John, Etuna, Eva-Liisa, Lahja and Fredy. Even though I did not stay long, only one and half years of teaching at the school, I enjoyed my time there. I left Iipumbu SSS in June 2004.

Ongwediva College of Education

It was one year after I had transferred to Iipumbu Senior Secondary School and I found an interesting post advertised at Ongwediva College of Education seeking a Lecturer for Human Movement Education. The candidate was expected to have done Physical Education at the institution of higher learning as one of the basic requirements. I did not hesitate to apply for the post. I was shortlisted for the interview and after that I was informed that I was the successful candidate.

I could not believe my luck when I received a call one day in the morning from the Head Office in Windhoek informing me that I was a successful candidate for the post of Human Movement Education module at Ongwediva College of Education. I jumped and I rejoiced at the news.

The first day I went to report for duty I remember I was taken to the office of the Rector *Meme* Babsy. She welcomed me warmly saying "George welcome to Ongwediva College, you are a young man and we need you to make a contribution." After a short while she called on her secretary to inform my Head of Department for him to come. When my HoD came he first shook my hand and invited me to follow him to his office. I could see he was a good soft-hearted man and soft spoken too. In his office he welcomed me to his department. He then gave me my subject syllabus and a book. He said that we would work hand in hand to support me before I could work on my own.

When we had finished talking and the orientation was over, we then went to the main staff room where we found some department colleagues waiting to welcome me. It was a wonderful hospitality. I was informed that I would use the common room as my office. There were two of us staying in the common room, my friend *Meme* Emma and I. The name of the department was called Skills Department. It was a department which consisted mainly of technical and skills subjects such as: HME, Arts Education, Home Science, Technical Studies and Commerce field of study.

I started Human Movement Education (HME) year 1 until I moved to year 3 level under the Basic Education Teacher Diploma (BETD) program. It was a three years program. There were three of us responsible for HME at each year level. We used to move with our students from year one till the last year three. I enjoyed teaching HME especially I liked more practical lessons, it was good. I was also given Integrated Media Technology Education (IMTE) module to teach and Business Management. I was in the best department.

Skills Department was the ideal and exemplary department for the entire college. We were one big family. As a department we used to work together as a family in many ways. There were social events like tea break where we used to come together and share a cup of tea in our department common room. There was an event known as the end of the term party.

We used to book at one of the local hotels and restaurants to have a moment to reflect and say good byes to one another. During those gatherings funny stories and jokes were shared, it was truly amazing moments. We could laugh at anything and everything. I worked at so many different places but I was never made to experience the same collegial relationship as compared to what we had in the Skills Department. I left Skills Department in December 2010 when the College merged with the University of Namibia.

University of Namibia Hifikepunye Pohamba Campus

I joined University of Namibia on January 2011 at Hifikepunye Pohamba Campus when all teacher training colleges merged with the University. I was appointed as a lecturer in the Department of Educational Psychology and Inclusive Education. It was a great opportunity.

As a Lecturer I taught modules such as Child development, Childhood Learning and Physical Education in my first two years after joining UNAM. I was then appointed to be a module leader of Guidance and counseling. Honestly speaking Guidance and counseling was my best module, I enjoyed lecturing at the university. I was passionate about the issues of Guidance and counseling, the theory and practice part of the module.

Being an academic, I was appointed as a co-supervisor in the department and I was given two Master students to co-supervise. I did my supervision duties to the best of my ability. I supported my students from writing their proposal, when they went to present their proposal to the department until they went to collect data. They were progressing successfully with their research projects. I was also responsible for reviewing faculty of Education proposals for approval.

Part of my job description was to meet the psychosocial needs of students through mentoring and counseling. I had many breakthroughs especially through counseling, there were many students who found it difficult to cope at the university but I helped them to see their way through. The issues I mostly dealt with were: teenage pregnancy, theft, alcohol and drug abuse, failing many modules and relationship problems. However, the good news was that most of the students became graduates and productive citizens through counseling intervention.

Sport wise, I was mainly coaching Volleyball teams. We usually had training sessions in the afternoon with both male and female students. There were many games and tournaments our students took part in and won. There was also a staff Volleyball team at the campus which I was responsible to organize with other staff members who loved Volleyball. We had played some games against students. Volleyball helped us to maintain fitness and health among us staff members.

I had wonderful memories of my time well spent at HPC ranging from my lectures and interaction with student teachers and colleagues like *Tate* Yakoop. *Tate* Yakoop and I were good friends, we joked and laughed out loud. Other colleagues that contributed positively toward my professional and personal development were: *Meme:* Helena, Emma, Lydia, Ottilie, Ndiina, Paulina, Victoria, Teopolina, Suama (my neighbor), Susan, Meameno, Soini, Erkning, Alina, Tulonga, Evelyne and *Tate:* Leonard, Massamba, Walter, Immanuel, Willem, Patoko, Asuguo, Amram, Kisco, Patrick, John, Ashili and Abed. We shared and learned open-mindedly from each other as colleagues. I was really good to everyone and everyone was good to me.

STEPPING INTO PUBLIC HEALTH CAREER PATH

This is what I call going back to the drawing board to look into a career path to say yes this is what I have been looking for all my life. I fairly believe that sometimes careers choose us when we do not have better resources and opportunity to choose the careers we truly want to follow with all our hearts. I also believe that when it happens that a career chooses you, the heart will not stop seeking for the right career.

Here in this section I talk more about my interest to step into public health sector. Ever since my childhood I have been always a health practitioner by choice. With the opportunities opening up for me, I now write about how I am slowly becoming a health practitioner by career. I am embarking on this public health journey and I will not leave it before I get to the top, that's to get my PhD in public health, one day soon. This is my overall ten year vision. But everything I have achieved in life I started from the humble beginning. I never took any short cuts. Let me now write about how I stepped into public health sector.

Doing Post-Doctorate Fellowship

Doing a post-doctorate in Faculty of Health Sciences came at the time I needed to expand my knowledge base and expertise. I felt inside me that I needed to go and do something to up-skill myself. It was like God was leading me after seeing my internal desire to go and get further education and training. I simply opened the Google search webpage, entered post-doctoral in educational psychology and the result was a call of a Post-Doctoral research fellowship advertised by the Faculty of Health Sciences of University of Fort Hare, my former university. I was very excited by the call which was on Mentoring for Sustainable Rural Community, Resilience and Public Health Niche Area. The closing date for applications was June 30, 2014. I did not waste anytime I sent my letter of application, accompanied by: the Title and Abstract of my doctoral thesis; a certified copy of my PhD degree certificate; a copy of passport document; a comprehensive curriculum vitae including list of publications and the names and contact details of my two referees.

It was not for long before I received a call from the School of Health Sciences telling me that I was invited to attend an interview for the Post-Doctoral Fellowship position I had applied for. Meanwhile I was in preparation to go for the interview I received an email from the Head of the School informing me that I was admitted and there was no need for the interview any more. I was very happy.

I went to one of my best former colleague and friend *Tate* Indongo whose office was next to mine to share my good news. He was equally happy for me and he wished me well. After a week or so I received another email with an attachment letter of admission. That day was my best moment ever! And then there were a number of calls and emails between the school Head and myself about when I should go and start my fellowship. At the time the admission letter came, I sent it to my department coordinator with my leave application.

Since I was not having a module in the first semester I asked if I could be away to do my fellowship which was only one year and to come back on the second semester to teach my module. I tried first to apply for the leave so that I would go and do my postdoctoral fellowship and return after my contract ended. But I came to learn that my application was not submitted to the relevant offices and the committee responsible for staff development. When I came back from South Africa I did not have any other choice but to resign from UNAM in October 2014.

Honestly speaking, my post-doctorate was a great opportunity for me which had changed my life in many ways as an academic. When I went to Fort Hare University I was told that I was placed under Dr. Mlisa whose office was based in Alice, the main campus. I first spent three months in a Bed and Breakfast facility before I went to my place of work which was supposed to be Tsengiwe village.

I was actually treated very well during my first three months in a Bed and Breakfast where I was accommodated. I was with Ms. Sande and her family.

They were extraordinary people, kind and full of understanding. My breakfast and super were always ready for me. I am a firm believer that when you are with happy people one becomes happy too. I was more than happy in East London. I was truly blessed to be with them and I enjoyed my stay very much.

The University especially the Faculty of Health Sciences supported me kindly. I was even provided with the university transport to and from work for a period of three months. I was told by the school head that I should just tell the driver to take me anywhere I wanted day and night. It was an amazing experience. We were admitted the two of us with my best friend Dr. Mbele as post-doctoral fellows.

We were given our staff cards together, an office and computer to do our work. Dr. Mbele being a South African citizen supported me in many ways especially at the time I was trying to open a bank account. He made my stay even worth living. Whenever I needed to go to town he was always ready to take me with his car. I did not know how I could have survived without my best friend Dr. Mbele. He was very kind and supportive from day one.

The only challenge I faced during the first three months of my post-doctorate was opening a bank account. Opening a local bank account was a basic requirement so that the university could pay me. The main contributing factor was that I did not have a permanent residence letter. The only letter I had was the letter for the Bed and Breakfast where I was temporarily accommodated. The bank people were ever saying the same thing "B n B is not a permanent residence my friend." I remember my friend Dr. Mbele and I had finished all the banks in East London without a single bank showing an interest to assist me open an account. It was a struggle full of disappointments and frustrations.

After three months in East London it was then the time to move supposed to Tsengiwe village in Cala. I never knew how the place looked like and where I would be staying. We made an appointment with the driver from the Faculty of Health Sciences Mr. Khaze to drive me early in the morning to go and see my work station Tsengiwe village. As we were driving along the way I started getting a bad feeling seeing how far the place was and the feelings of frustration started kicking in. And then I asked the driver, how far we still had to drive. His response was between 100 Kilometers more. I never liked Mr. Khaze, the driver's response at all.

I was just there in the car on the back seat thinking, village boy where are you going with this man? What kind of place is this Tsengiwe village? After a while on the road we stopped to fill up fuel in one town. After some long drives I saw a road sign which read 10 Kilometers to Cala and the driver quickly remarked, soon we are there Dr. Out of frustration I pretended I never heard what he said.

Then before Cala town the driver turned left side following the handwritten sign Tsengiwe. By then we left the tarred road driving toward the village in the sand and rocky road. I was starting to get lost in my imagination thinking how on beautiful world to stay in such a faraway village, but I was still saying let me not think too much, too early and too quickly. As the driver was driving I kept on looking around near and far to find something that would fascinate me but to my surprise there was more disappointment coming my way.

The picture of Tsengiwe village was that, it was like an island or a desert, it was an open space from the beginning to the end. I could see animals grazing far in the area over miles. It was a typical beautiful and yet rural village. I was day dreaming about living there but deep down my whole being was against me living there. After some driving the driver informed me "Dr. here we are, this is the office where you will be based." He was talking as he was opening the car door, coming out.

I was still stuck on the car seat surprised and totally confused. I had endless questions to ask but how could I ask them, Mr. Khaze was just the innocent driver, no. I swallowed my pride and opened the door and I came out of the car. Looking at the center which I was invited to come and work I knew it was not possible to accept that offer. Staff working at the center who were informed about my visit welcomed us warmly and I started introducing myself, my name and where I came from. I knew I had lied because I said I like the office and the surrounding. We only found a building made out of sand and water by the community volunteers and I did not think it was safe enough.

After my visit at the office and its surrounding, the driver and one of the staff working at the office Mr. Petty made an arrangement to go to Cala Municipality office to get me a letter of permanent residence that I would use to open my bank account. On our way to the office Mr. Petty was telling me that he knew Namibia and liked our country. He was kind enough to get me the letter with a stamp and a signature. I thanked him from bottom of my heart for having done that in order to open my bank account. After we got the letter from the municipality office, I went quickly to the First National Bank to see if I could open an account. When I got inside the bank it was still a disappointment. I thought after getting a permanent residence letter my problem was solved but there was another problem in my passport. The beautiful lady who had asked me to provide her with the necessary documents gave me the bad news that as a foreigner the bank needs a valid work permit or a visa. The next problem was then with a work permit. After I convinced her that I was a post-doctoral researcher employed on contract I was given a study permit but not a work permit.

She called the branch manager and when he came he looked at me like I have done something wrong and he asked me rudely "Where is your work permit because this is not a South African passport." Before I answered him I was thinking why did I come to South Africa to be treated like that? I felt very bad and disappointed. I showed him that I had a valid study permit which was due to expire in December 2014. And that was exactly where the problem was, he clearly pointed out that as a bank they could not open an account with a study permit not valid for a minimum of three months. I said it was okay, I thanked him and I left the bank.

The driver Mr. Khaze was seated in the car waiting for me. I just said let us go and leave this place. He never asked me if I succeeded opening an account and I also did not tell him. I got the feeling that he could see that I was grieving. I was totally disappointed because I knew that I would not get any money in the next three to four months before I got the valid study permit. As I was seated in the car I was planning to go back to Namibia so that I could apply for my study permit. I had so many things going on in my mind; about my life, my children and my future.

On our way back to Alice town I kept on saying: "No, No, No, not me". I kept on saying No, No, many times thinking about me living in Tsengiwe village, the treatment I got from the bank, the study permit and opening an account, oh it was just too much for me. I wished I was already in Alice to cry all that loud out. I just needed to be alone and cry my heart out. I never knew that the driver heard me when I kept on saying No, no, he said "Are you okay Doctor"? He was very sympathetic with me and he started warning me that I should not agree to live in that village because it was far and I would suffer there. I agreed and promised him that I would not come back to stay there. He was really trying to lift me up. He gave me some best options to think about. One of those option was when we mutually agreed that it would be better for me to only come at the Centre two or three days in a week and go back on the same day. He said that way it would be much better. I felt it was a good idea. We arrived in Alice town very well and the driver drove back to East London where he stayed.

I should make it clear that there was nothing wrong with Tsengiwe village. On the contrary the village was very beautiful and looked peaceful. There were many development projects and activities. The village had a school and a clinic. I only felt personally that I was not quite prepared mentally how I would get an opportunity to learn and expand my knowledge while living in the village. It was a difficult for me to accept living there wholeheartedly while I came to gain research knowledge and skills and yet the environment seemed not to be the right one.

After I arrived at the lodge where I was staying, I wrote an e-mail to give a feedback to the head of School of Health Sciences about my trip. I proposed to be based in Alice and I would have some days in a week to work at the Centre in Tsengiwe village. I showed my interest to work sometimes in the school to gain knowledge and skills. I also shared that I needed to apply for a study permit, I therefore requested her if I could go back to Namibia the following day. She responded positively that the arrangement was good and then she reminded me to communicate with my direct supervisor.

I managed to go back home in December 2014 to apply for study permit. I was satisfied with the service I received from both South African Embassy and Namibian Police in Windhoek. It took me about three weeks to get my study permit finalized and issued. When it was done while I was in the village, I asked one of my friend Aletta to collect it for me from the Embassy. With all documents available by then I opened my bank account first week I got back to South Africa in January 2015. Everything started to go accordingly. It was after two days when I arrived back in Alice I went to see my supervisor to update her with regard to my study permit and to start with my contract.

Even though my supervisor wanted me to stay in Tsengiwe, her home village at least she agreed that it was okay for me to stay in Alice. She gave me an office in Alice campus situated in Student Counseling Unit building near the university's main gate. She made me sign my job description that specifically aiming to develop a community center in Tsengiwe village. She was very passionate about the community center's development. I could see that the center had a lot of potential to develop in terms of infrastructure wise and staff capacity development.

It was therefore part of my job description to capacitate the staff working at the center with research skills to publish findings of the projects they were doing in the community. I was also assigned to provide technical and professional assistance to HIV and AIDS unit at the university. I learned a lot about the seven programs that the Unit was responsible offering to the university community.

HIV and AIDS Unit was implementing Higher Education and Training HIV/AIDS (HEAIDS) seven programs which included: Curriculum integration program, Future Beat Radio and Social Media Program, Alcohol and abuse prevention program, Women's Health and Empowerment Program, Men having Sex with Men/Lesbian Bisexual Transgender and Intersexed program, First Things First, Men's Health and Empowerment Program. These programs were implemented in all three UFH campuses namely: Alice, Bisho and East London.

HIV/AIDS Unit organized the World AIDS day on the 1st of December 2014 where I also addressed the community with the message of support and hope. The event was well attended by Tsengive community. We also went to launch Zazi Know Your Strength Program at Tsengiwe village a program targeting adolescent girls in the community to teach them about resilience.

As a post-doctorate fellow, I organized and co-facilitated a Research Writing Seminar to capacitate the staff working at the community center in Tsengiwe village under Indigenous Knowledge Systems (IKS) and mentored them on research processes from collecting data, analyzing, presentation, discussion and conclusion for possible publication. We had an incredible week of hard work with my co-facilitator Prof. Nicodem. It was also a great opportunity for me to learn how to facilitate a research writing seminar.

Talking of personal development opportunities, there were many workshops offered by the University of Fort Hare under Govan Mbeki Research and Development Center. I attended workshops on: How to become a good supervisor, writing grant applications, project financial management and budgeting, how to analyze qualitative and quantitative data among others.

Not only that, I had opportunity to work with the Nursing Sciences Department on projects grant applications. One of the example was a project on School Health Policy which was funded by South African Medical Research Council (MRC). I learned quite a lot as a researcher especially how to write a project proposal for funding and work collaboratively in a research team.

The Faculty of Health Sciences had organized a one full week workshop on writing for publication. It was a workshop well-facilitated by the most highly recognized Professors in South African universities. I learned a great deal step by step how to write a paper for publication.

One of my key job description was to publish at least two articles in one of accredited and recognized journals. I managed to publish three journal articles and one book chapter during my post-doctorate. My contract ended in September 2015. Before my contract ended I applied for Masters in Public Health program better known as Albertina Sisulu Executive Leadership Program in Health (ASELPH) offered by the University of Fort Hare in the Faculty of Health Sciences. The program was designed for South African Executive Leaders to improve South African public health sector.

I was very lucky to receive a call of admission to the program. I knew very well that being a Namibian it was a lifetime opportunity to get my name chosen under a program that was specifically targeting only South African executive leaders at public health facilities. It is truly a blessing and I am working hard toward obtaining my second Masters degree.

Doing Masters in Public Health

ASELPH is a partnership amongst the University of Pretoria, the University of Fort Hare, Harvard School of Public Health and South Africa Partners in collaboration with the South African National and Provincial Departments of Health. The program specifically aims to strengthen human resource capacity in the health system needed to deliver high quality, cost-efficient services through executive-level training of health leaders and managers. ASELPH is envisioned as a local 'flagship programme' capable of setting the standard for executive level health leadership and management training in South Africa.

Even though I am not a South African citizen I found ASELPH as a powerful tool to transform me from Education background to Health sector. In the program the electives I specialize in is Health Research namely: Epidemiology, Advanced Epidemiology and Biostatistics. I started with the program in 2015 and I would finish in 2017. My future aspiration is to continue pursuing my PhD in Public Health in the near future.

THE DAY I GOT MARRIED

The date 17 August 2006 will never be just an ordinary day for me. That was the date I married a beautiful woman Fransina from Iikokola village. We had two marriage ceremonies that became necessary because the Pastor at Elombe Church was not licensed to issue a marriage certificate by then.

Therefore, our first marriage ceremony was officiated by Pastor Joseph Avia in Gloria Day Church in Ongwediva in the presence of our best man and best woman Mr. and Mrs. Haihambo. Our second marriage ceremony was officiated by Pastor Debora Nuuyoma at Elombe Elcin Church in front of our two families, bridesmaids, friends and colleagues on August 26, 2006.

My best friend Tobby was our driver to and from church. During the ceremony, my favorite part was when we finished our vows and the Pastor informed me "Now you can kiss your bride" I was like, Oh My God! I could not do it in front of such a big crowd and come on, it was even in the church, a place where God was directly watching my every move. I enjoyed that event very much.

I was equally impressed to see my very good friends and colleagues coming to witness my big day. Among my colleagues that came were Dr. Rev Iita, *Meme*. Helena, Susan, Lydia, *Tate*. Abed and Yakoop. They just made my day even better and memorable. In our marriage God blessed us with three beautiful children; Tangi-Hope (daughter) born in 2007, Tanga-Happy (Son) born in 2008 and Tunga-Home Georgia (daughter) born in 2012.

AGAINST ALL ODDS

Didn't you hear people saying you can achieve anything you want in life and that you can be anyone you want to become? Or something like, dream big and your dream can become a reality. Or statements like, the sky is the limit. Or an advice that says it is not about who your parents are or where you were born, blessings get to you no matter who you are or where you were born. This section is all about that to demonstrate how life has been for me the poor boy facing many challenges in my search for a better future.

I deliberately put this section at the center of this book because this is the heart of my life journey. I forever feel this section deeply down in my heart, it is the center of my life story. As a poor village boy I struggled throughout my life to get what I needed most without giving up. You know what, when I was a little boy my arm was fractured and both of my legs were kicked and fractured in the game of soccer.

I was even kicked on my head during one of soccer matches at Oshali village which resulted into a serious head injury. I was a goal keeper when *the* incident happened and it was my last time behind the goal posts. I was between heaven and earth until some old women came with boiled water to give me a second chance to live. When I was taken to the hospital I never knew how it happened up until today I just came to learn from stories, I was unconscious to tell the truth. I survived all those incidents and here I am writing the story of my life.

Even as young as 8 years I fell in that borehole full of broken bottles, I came out bleeding with a pool of blood all over my body, almost half dead and I was taken to the hospital. It was a deadly scene but I survived that. I think by now you may have funny ideas that I have a life for a cat or you may simply want to call me a man of many lives. I survived too many things and to me that is a blessing. I am highly blessed and favored. That is a story of a refugee boy.

I remember when I was just thirteen years deciding to go to war to liberate our country Namibia. Our dear *Meme* Ndateelela came to stop us from going to war. We did not abandon the idea, we decided to go the same night and we went. We walked miles and miles in deep woods of both Namibia and Angola, day and night until we arrived at a pick up point inside Angola. I was the youngest among big boys, I overcame whatever was in my way to cross the borders.

It was even worse throughout my education journey. For example when I was at the secondary school my name was always on the list of the learners that did not pay the school fees. I remember I was nearly left out to write my Grade 10 National final examination due to lack of money to pay. I was lucky my father came from Oranjemund town where he used to work and I did not know who told him that there were only three days left for me to pay examination. I was just in our hostel room and one of the learners came running to inform me that my father was at the gate asking for me. When I went to see him I told him the situation and he gave me the money to pay the same day. That day is still fresh in my mind, it is just like it happened yesterday. Finally, I paid for my examination and I passed Grade 10 and life went on. I was in Grade 11 the following academic year.

Even my Grade 12 final examination my name was also listed among the few learners who did not pay for their exam. We were given only a week, meaning five working days to settle or else we would not be allowed to write the final exam. That time it was even tougher for me, choices and sources were just too limited. I did not know what to do. Writing a letter to my father it would take months to get to him and I did not know even his postal address. And even if I knew his postal address, how on earth would I post that letter and where? It could never happen that time. Truth be told I also did not know my father's work telephone number to call him and even if I knew his telephone number where would I get the money to call him.

I did not have any means to do anything. I was just in the hostel quiet and most of my friends did not know what was going on in my life. But for me I knew it, it was poverty. I knew it from the day I was born that I was born by a poor woman who never worked in her entire life, a village woman who did not go to school to learn how to read and write and she died poor, so nothing was new to me by that time. I was just saying I am used to this thing called poverty but I vowed that my children will not go through the same thing.

At the very last minute I remembered that my maternal grandmother was receiving an old age pension. I decided to ask for permission from school to go to Ongombeyaola village with the hope to ask my grandmother for some money to pay for my Grade 12 examination. Since the school was aware about my name being in the list I was given a permission to go and look for money to pay my exam. So I went.

I found my grandmother in her small home which comprised of two huts sitting busy weaving the traditional basket. I politely greeted her and told her that I missed her very much. My grandmother was my pillar of strength and served as my last resort. Whenever things got tougher my grandmother popped up in my mind and she never disappointed me.

To cut a long story short I then informed grandma about my predicament of my lack of money to pay for the examination. She sadly told me that *"Simon George shiveli ina tukwata manga opo handi mono oshimaliwa"* literally means that she did not receive her pension as yet and she did not have money. After she honestly told me that, I started crying so badly, I just lied on the ground next to her crying and crying. She was deeply touched emotionally and felt sorry for me. I knew she would never forget that moment even today as she was resting in her grave peacefully. I cried hard. Tears were flooding all over my face towards my entire body. She was pleading so that I stop crying: "It is enough now please stop."

She brought me a cup of water to drink and she promised me that she would find a way to help me. She said stand up let us go to one of a Samaritan woman on the other side of oshana. So we went, I came to learn that the Samaritan woman was a teacher and she used to assist my grandma financially many times. We went in her coca shop, luckily enough we found her there. My grandma asked if they could talk in private outside her shop. After few minutes they came back and I saw her giving my grandma some money and we left for my grandma's home after that.

When we got home she handed me the money and she promised me that when she got her pension she would pay back our Samaritan woman. By then I was at peace I could not wait to get to school to pay for my examination. The following day came I went to the office I paid and got myself a ticket to write my exam.

That year 1994 was not my year at all. Just three weeks to start writing my final examination I got sick. It was very serious, I had stomach ache, a severe pain and it was like I had a virus burning me inside my stomach. Days were coming closer and closer to the examination and I was not getting better. I left the hostel to go stay with my late aunt Saima my mother's sister in Okapumbu village. It was not far from the school. I was severely in pain. I had something in my stomach moving towards my heart like something sharp cutting me.

Surprisingly, I was informed by my cousin that the following day other learners would be writing English oral examination and the next day would be Oshikwanyama oral examination. I thought I would wake up ready to go for examination, I could not manage. My cousin Justus put me on the bicycle but just a few miles from home I started vomiting and became very weak. We then decided it was better he took me back home. I never sat for any oral examinations for the two languages.

When the normal examination started, it started with Agriculture subject by then I was not in severe pain as before but I was still very weak. I went to write but I could not finish answering all the questions. The other first term and mid-term examinations I was on top of the class taking number 1 spot, it was actually my class as far as best class performance was concerned. I still remember it was Grade 12 G class of 1994. The final examination continued with the rest of the subjects. By then I started recovering very well and I even came back in the hostel. In the end when the national results were announced publically my name was among those learners who passed Grade 12. I had made it and I was so happy.

Then coming to the University of Namibia as a student. The same thing, same challenge of settling examination fees reappeared. I only survived my first year 1996 of study without having my name on the list of students who were asked to settle their debts. I was fortunate enough to be awarded a study bursary of N$12000 per year by the Government of Namibia. However as the study periods went on more courses were added which took up so much money than the bursary amount could cover.

The following second year my name was in the list to settle my debts before I was allowed to write examination. That year our Student Representative Council fought for us as poor students not to be denied the opportunity to write our examination. The university understood to wave our fees. I therefore survived that year.

My third year it was the same thing my name was in the list and the university decided that every student must pay before entering examination hall. The university council was not prepared to discuss or wave the student debts that year. I was in big dilemma, where would I get the money to settle the debt. I remember I had about N$ 6000-00 to settle.

The question I had was, where would I get such amount to pay so that I would write my examination? The idea of grandmother came in my mind, of course I knew she would not afford that with her pension of only N$100-00 she could not do anything and she was 800 Kilometers away in the far Northern part of the country. Settling deadlines were coming nearer and nearer and yet I did not find a solution.

Then boom! The idea came up in my mind to go to the Finance Department and talk to people there about my situation. I went right away straight to the Finance Department, it was in the late afternoon and the staff was about to leave. When I got there I asked the secretary if I could talk to somebody in the department to help me. The secretary told me that it was late they were about to leave for home and that I should come in the morning the following day. Then the following day was Wednesday when I went there. I was told Wednesday was not a students' consultation day I should go and come back either on Thursday or Monday or Tuesday. I said to her but madam you told me yesterday that I should come back today now you are telling me this again. She defended herself and said in her Afrikaans that *"Is jy nie ons universiteit student ken jou dae om finasiële departement raadpleeg"?* Literally means that are you not our university student to know which days to consult Finance Department? I left very disappointed.

The following day I was there again and the same lady asked me "Who do you exactly want to see here?" I was straight forward, I said madam I am a poor student and I want to talk to somebody who can help understand my situation. While I was explaining to her, a white lady came out of one of the offices she said tell that student to come to me. I went in her office, her name was Mrs. English.

Looking at her she was a lovely and motherly lady. I told her my situation that I was very poor I could only come to study at the university because of the Government bursary and that I did not have any other financial source to help me settle my debts. She was telling me encouraging words that I should not worry all she needed was just to write down my name and to sign a form so that the money would be transferred from my next year bursary. As I was about to leave her office she said Simon you must promise me that you will work hard in your studies. I said I will work hard *meme*. From that moment there I had found my friend and my God mother.

My fourth year (final year) it was still the same thing I owed the university and my name was displayed with the same message no examination entry before settling the debts. I did not hesitate to go to my God mother Mrs. English. I knocked at her door and she was in the office. I explained to her and she said to me it was then difficult because I was in the final year, meaning there would be no more bursary money coming in. We then agreed that I would use my first and second months' salary as a teacher to settle for my debts. In the end she was kind to me and suggested that I should just make sure all debts were settled before April so that I could graduate.

I did exactly that, my first three months' salary I used it to settle for my university debts. When the graduation day came I was in the suit and tie walking tall and proud with my name in the graduation list of the year 2000 Bachelor of Education Degree. How resilient and successful story that was!

I know you may ask how is it possible having gone through those hardships and yet I succeeded in life. It is called resilience and self-determination. I have faith too and I am a firm believer in God's blessings. Even though I know that I am a poor orphan boy I know I am a child of God and that is good motivation to overcome whatever is presented in front of me. I know at the end I will survive it. Like I always say in the end I will overcome it no matter how difficult the situation might be.

Studying for my Masters and PhD in South Africa was even more challenging as a foreign student. For a start I should say that as an international full-time student I needed to apply for the study leave from my employer at that time. To say the least that was a huge battle I faced to finally get my study leave approved. That experience has taught me that some people are not happy to see others advancing in life.

Equally I needed the study permit where there were many offices I visited before I finally got my study permit. It was a very frustrating and lengthy process. Documents such as university admission letter, letter of accommodation, detail of financial study support, police clearance and a valid passport were required to complete the study permit application.

For the Master program I first faced the adjustment issues being away from home and my dear family. One particular challenge that deserves special mentioning happened in one of the research seminars we had at Bisho Campus where we were expected to write our research topics, statement of the problem, research questions, objectives and significance of the study.

When one of the facilitators came to look at what I did he slashed my proposal down with no mercy whatsoever. He said that my topic was not a researchable topic. He suggested I should think of something else to do and not the topic I came up with. He then left without showing an interest in my work at all. I felt so small and behind. I called him again after a few corrections where he said to me "Simon leave this thing you are doing there is no research there." I was very embarrassed.

I stopped doing anything and I went outside for some fresh air. It was not true, I went outside to cry and asked myself if I should pack my bags and go back to Namibia. On our way back to Alice campus, other students that were with me in the University bus started asking me what was wrong and why I was angry and looked worried during the seminar. I never responded a single word to what they were asking. When we finally arrived in our study room my friend Ruben sat me down and helped me with a research topic. From that moment everything was cleared. I never changed the topic again, my friend had helped me. In the end I did my research on the same topic and I graduated in record period.

Doing my PhD was another difficult period. First of all I enrolled one year before all teacher colleges were merging with UNAM. There were just too many issues at the campus level that I could not get an approved study leave. I decided that I would register as a full time while I was still employed full time doing my work. I arranged with my project supervisor that I would spend two to three weeks in South Africa every month. To tell the truth there was a departmental Coordinator whom we did not see eye to eye with and that made my study life very difficult. I spoke to my supervisor about all her ill motives to stop me from progressing with my studies and the supervisor encouraged me to forget about her and focus primarily on my study.

The most difficult challenge I faced during PhD studies was lack of accommodation. I asked other student colleagues at that time if I could sleep in the study room/office. They all understood my situation and agreed to let me use one of the office rooms to do my work and as my bedroom as well. It was good because I spent most of the time working on the computer and few hours of sleeping. My motto was sleeping will never give me my doctorate. I started first sleeping on the floor with the support of boxes. It was only then I bought a single mattress to use. I used to wake up early in the morning to go to one of the hostels for bathing.

My difficult situation only encouraged me to work hard. Before anyone noticed I was done with my studies within one and half year period. Most of the students who were sleeping in luxury accommodation and studying full-time with nothing else to do were surprised to learn that I completed my studies. When the graduation list was officially announced in 2012 two years after I had registered, my name was listed to graduate with a PhD. Then my graduation day challenge again. I survived a deadly scene during the day of my graduation. I was nearly killed to tell the honest truth.

I should say that day did not start on a positive note, I survived a deadly scene. It happened in the morning behind the Bed and Breakfast Guesthouse where I spent the night in King William's Town, South Africa. I had to wake up early in the morning to catch the first transport to Alice town where the graduation was held.

I was carrying my suite case and my gown in both arms (a suite case on one arm and my gown on the other arm). I just saw two gentlemen moving towards me. Looking at their dirty hair and old clothing they wore, I felt that I was in danger. They spoke something in IsiXhosa which I could not pick up, things were happening so fast. All of a sudden one of them was standing in front of me and one behind me. The one behind me kicked my legs and I found myself lying on the ground and when I looked up at them I saw them holding sharp long knives and I heard a sound of a car passing by with a loud shout. By then I was half dead, Oh My God!

After a few seconds I could see I was still alive but I never saw what happened to the men who were holding knives pointing at me. God is truly great, I had survived and I had to stand up to go to the bus stop. As I was walking to the bus stop I kept on looking in all directions until I finally got there safe. Then I started narrating my ordeal to the other passengers in the bus. While I was doing that there was an old lady in the bus who said something that caught my attention. She said "My son God loves you and He is with you". When I told them it was my graduation day, they all felt so sorry for me until I almost cried.

What was important however I managed to arrive safely and I went through the graduation proceedings successfully until I got my degree in my hand the same day. I knew that God was seeing everything that was happening and He made sure nothing would stop me. That is why I am proud of myself for being focused and determined to achieve my goals. Becoming a PhD holder I was not surprised at all since it was always my dream to get ahead in life for the love of education.

Nearly in everything I have accomplished in life there were always barriers and hurdles to jump. You have already read about how I transferred from Oshimwaku to Iipumbu Senior Secondary School, it was tough but in the end I went through it successfully. I even received a phone call from the Inspector of Education asking me to go back to Oshimwaku. I never went back, I stayed at Iipumbu and left it again. When I had to leave Iipumbu to Ongwediva College of Education some people wanted to stop me too but in the end I survived it.

And then there was my wedding again. During the preparation of my wedding ceremony, everything else was well in order. Just on the Friday morning on which the wedding ceremony was scheduled to take place, the next day my car windows were broken and money which I had left in the car was stolen. The entire suitcase which included all my bridesmaids' gowns and shoes was gone. Even my page boy suit and shoes were all gone.

My uncle went to the police station to open a case while we were trying to trace the person who had stolen my things. So much money was spent and so much money was wasted. We never recovered even a single gown, all the effort that was invested was in vein. I drove back to the lady *Meme* Helen who helped me with gowns to at least make something for my page boy to wear. I could see they had a lot of orders and her employees were overwhelmed. The good news was that Saturday came I was in the Elombe Elcin Church for our wedding day on the 26 August 2006 and I married my wife. Funny part was that my wife and I were driven in the same car with a broken window. That was how determined I was. Nothing could stop me, I survived it. In the end I always survive it.

I also wish to relate the story of the birth of my daughter Tangi Hope. When her mother was ready to deliver, I took her early in the morning to the hospital. We were there since 4:00 AM and my wife was told that she was in labour. She was told that she had to walk around the ward since the child was still far and all that. After some few hours there was no progress and we were told to go back home. Around 10:00 we went back home. By noon my wife was crying out of pain again saying I should take her back to the hospital. I had to drive her back.

When we got there, her doctor came around 14:15 and she was still not ready to deliver the child. She was put in one of the consultation rooms and around past 16:00 or so her doctor informed her that the last option was to go to the theater to save the life of our dear child. I was told to go home and the nurse would call me. I refused, after all I was the father of the child and that was my wife about to deliver our first child. I decided that I was not going anywhere. Then one nurse came to me and convinced me that it would not be easy for me to go to the operating room. I then said fine and left. She said it was a good decision for my benefit.

I was just walking around the hospital like a psychiatric patient. It was an emotional scene I will never forget. Later on after two hours or more I got a call that my baby girl and her mother were all well and I should go to see them. It was not easy at all but in the end we survived that. In my entire life that is how things have been unfolding but in the end I manage to survive. I am that boy, brave and courageous. If I decide that I want something I will get it, no matter how far it is or how big and I will. In that way I think I am blessed.

In 2014 the Faculty of Health Sciences of the University of Fort Hare in East London, invited me to go and do my Post-Doctoral fellowship. I applied for the leave from UNAM and my application was put aside and could not be submitted to the responsible committee for approval. When I came back from South Africa I just told myself I was resigning. I resigned and left to go and do what I needed to do for my life without looking back. I am like that, I follow my heart at all cost. Many people did not approve of my decision and labeled me many things. It hurt me to see people that I cared for doing that to me but I had a dream and I could see beyond that decision. After all I am just a human being living my life purposefully and honestly. Overall anyone can see that whatever challenges I faced, they never deterred me from achieving my education goals. I am proud to say in the end I got BEd, PGDSE, MEd, PhD, Post-Doctorate and I am in the final year to complete my second Masters in Public Health. How colorful is that!

In closing, the key message here ladies and gentlemen under this section 'Against all odds' which also happens to be the theme of this book is what I call a story of RESILIENCE. In their book chapter Dap Louw, Norman Duncan, Linda Richter and Anet Louw talk of resilience as: The ability to 'bounce back' from or adjust effectively to risky life factors. This is exactly what this book is all about, a resilience story of my life and my ability to bounce back from many risky life factors I endured in my life starting from the day I was born, growing up, my education, my career and my family (noting that all my parents and grandparents are all dead) but look at me.

MY HAPPY MOMENTS

I had many happy moments throughout my life journey. This section is especially dedicated to those moments when I had really good times. I am generally a happy person and my smile is what I am known for. If there is a day I don't have a smile on my face usually people will keep on asking what is wrong and why I am not happy. These moments are not in any particular order but I should say perhaps they all have equal significance and value in my life.

When I was a second best learner

The first happy moment I remember took place in 1984 when I was 10 years old at the time I came second in grade 3 and my cousin Indileni came number one in the class. I vividly remember it was in the Omundudu Church where the school used to give the reports at the end of the school term. What made it special was the presence of our grandfather Gabriel Taukeni.

I had a feeling how proud our grandfather was to see us his grandchildren being called following each other position number 1 and 2. Indileni is the first born of my father's twin sister *Meme* Kaleinasho Kandoshe and I am also my father's first born child. It was indeed a proud moment. We were walking in front of the church gathering to get our reports, tall and proud as children of the same blood. I will never forget that moment.

When I was a third best learner

Another happy moment took place in 1989 at Nyango Education Center in Zambia. I was in Form IV and I took a third position in the class. What made it special was when I was called by a surprise in front of all refugee girls and boys to get an award. It was very special.

The year 1989 was a special year for most people who were in exile for the liberation of Namibia. Many people who were of voting age were preparing to go to Namibia for elections and there I was receiving an award for the third best student in our class, how special. I was hoping that they would go and tell my family and friends that Simon is in Zambia and is doing very well in school. It was a very special recognition, happening at the right place and at the right moment.

My first day in the airplane

My first day in the airplane was in 1988 from Lubango Airport to Kwanza Sul, Angola. I was 14 years old. The night before our first ever flight as students in Lubango was a long one. I am sure we did not sleep that night out of excitement and fear of unknown. We were telling each other stories of how to be in airplane and how we should behave. I remember we were telling each other things we never even experienced or knew at that time.

One particular story was about people vomiting in the airplane and boy I became a victim. I vomited so badly during the takeoff and even somewhere up in the air after the plane had made some movement. It was a very special moment. I could see people walking up and down but I was scared to even move my leg. It was unbelievable, I had mixed feelings of fear and excitement.

The landing was also not a pleasant one, the plane took some time before landing and when it did my heart never stopped pounding. And then we were ushered where to take our bags and we went in a big truck with a group of soldiers. While we were on the road, there were some nice jeep cars that were driven very fast. Apparently they were there for communication. We were very fascinated by how we were driven and protected. We were singing SWAPO songs throughout our journey until we finally arrived in Luanda Civilian Center. It was a great place.

When I was number one best learner

It was in 1994 the Mid-Term results I was in Grade 12 and I did exceptionally well in the exam. It came first as a surprise because our reports were not given at the school assembly. The school only called some learners who took the second and third positions. Our names were only called out to go the office after the school assembly.

We were wondering asking ourselves what went wrong and so on. When we went in the office it was indeed a great surprise, we were told that you did very well and we deserved a special recognition. We were given some money as a recognition of our best performance. We were happy. That day was my happiest moment for ever.

My graduation day

It was on the 19th of May 2012, day of my graduation as Doctor of Philosophy. It was an incredible and memorable day for me. I never felt that way ever in my life. I was on cloud nine, a feeling of reaching a self-actualization. I know very well not many people would ever get an opportunity to have such a feeling of accomplishment.

I first took a trip from King Williams Town where I spent a night to Alice town where the graduation was taking place. The trip was very short just in few minutes we had arrived in Alice town. I put myself together and I went to one of the offices we usually use during our studies. The office of my supervisor was also just next door. I knocked at her door to see her before we moved to the hall. She was happy to see me and she told me to go change and wear my gown. The time was almost there to move to the hall, we were about six of us to be crowned as DRs; Jenny, Severious, Joyce, Faith, Wendy and myself. It was a colorful day.

It was like in a dream, the master of ceremony saying this is the time we all have been waiting for, let us call on Simon George, the graduate. I found myself standing next to my supervisor while she was reading my mini autobiography, I was just there standing tall and proud thinking that my father just got a son with a Ph.D. It was indeed a great moment that will always have a special place in my heart. Next page I pay tribute to my late parents and I wish you take time to read it.

TRIBUTE TO MY PARENTS

If it were not for my parents I would not be here writing this book that's why in this section I would like to pay special homage to my late parents who could not be here to taste the fruits of their support and sacrifices.

To my father: First of all is a tribute to my father George Mandume, my king. My father was one of the creative and gifted men I came to know. He lived his life to the fullest and he was loved by many people. He was friendly, funny, honest and sociable. He could make jokes that could even break ones ribs and/ or give one a stomachache out of laughter. I for one enjoyed his company and I miss him dearly.

My dad was a visionary man too. He had a vision for how and where he lived his life. My dad was very proud of us his children and we were proud of him too. He had a vision for me, his son. He saw my life what I would become at the time I was still a small boy. He said to me, "son you will grow up to be a responsible, wise and an educated man." I never really believed him until the day I graduated with my first degree. His absence in my life made me to think about his vision for me. He left me with his words that I will be responsible, wise and an educated man. He had that vision for me and I believed him.

I listened to people speaking so well of my father. I always wanted to be like him to be good with people and help the poor in the little way possible. My father liked to dress to impress and he had a car and a beautiful house which made him even famous in the village by then. He used to speak good English too, which made people in the village to start calling him an English man, *Omwiingilisha.* Professionally speaking, my father was a trained Carpenter and a licensed Electrician. He practiced his technical expertise in all spheres of life. My father was also a great sportsman. He enjoyed boxing, athletics, volleyball, squash and darts. He was very good at sport. The house was full of his medals and trophies that he had won in several competitions. He was such a sport man.

The death of my father in June 2000. When the news came, my siblings and I were in the sitting room about to watch the eight o'clock evening news on Namibian Broadcasting Corporation (NBC) Television. Nobody told us in words, we picked it from the hoot of a car. I remember saying to my siblings that "Daddy is gone, daddy is gone." It was heart breaking, shocking and devastating. I had been mourning my daddy throughout my life, there is not even a single day passing by without a thought of him running through my mind.

My father died in the same year I started working as a university graduate and I had not yet settled down to fully support him. It was a missed opportunity and it was too late to say thank you daddy for all your support. During the funeral I had a serious headache, I remember leaving for home to sleep before the end of the burial service. It was a very bad moment. I think I was worried so much about where I would be living after the death of my father. I was only left in God's hand to show me where my life would be after the passing of my dear dad. May your soul rest in eternal peace my dear dad.

To my mother: My mother, the queen of my heart her name was Maria Mwaifanange Namatwi Kalola. Most of my maternal family know her by the name Namatwi. When there were family events some of the elder family people introduced me as a child of Namatwi. I did not like people calling my mother that name. Namatwi is an Oshiwambo name meaning a person with big ears. To me as I remember my mother, she was born to be an African model. She was tall, with short black hair and a little bit of big beautiful ears.

When my mother died in 1992 it was the shock of my life. One of my cousins Justus brought the news to me at the school. When my cousin came to tell me the news I was in the hostel at Eengendjo SSS. When he came in our room I never thought that he came with a bad news. He just said Simon George let us go behind the hostel I want to tell you something important.

I remember we sat behind the school dining hall. After sitting, out of curiosity I asked him, is everything okay my brother? He then said that "Yeah everything is ok. But Simon, you know that your mother has not been well at home, we received the news that she passed on." I was speechless. I was just looking at him and I started crying. I leaned on his shoulders as I was crying.

After a while when he had finished consoling me and allowed me to take it all in, he asked me if there was something I needed to get from my room. I said I did not want to get anything let us just go home.

When we arrived home we first went to see my grandmother who was sitting inside the hut. We greeted her and she started telling us how my mother died. Part of what grandmother told us was that my mother was not feeling well and her condition took a turn for the worst at night following her death. She was supposed to be taken to the clinic in the morning but God had other plans for her life. She died at home and was buried the same day without a coffin and a proper funeral. I confess I never grew up with my mother but she has been always that queen of my heart. I have a special place in my heart for my mom. She was a tall and sexy young woman I came to love as a mother. She was very strong to carry me until the day she gave birth to me. I am proud of her. May her soul rest in peace.

To my great-grandmother: My great grandma Eunike *Mukwamalanga* Mokaxwa was a strong, resilient and persistent woman. She was a powerful woman who brought me up and taught me how to cook, clean, wash, plough and pound omahangu. She was the first person who taught me all the house chores. Her love for me as her grandson was undoubtedly shown and known by all.

When it was time to eat with big boys like uncles Aron, Sheehama, Stefa and other boys from the village, my grandma used to say "Simon George *shiveli tula kolumosho.*" It means that during the war we were taught to put some food on the left hand in case something happens at least one could run with food on the other hand. And also thinking that those big boys would eat up all the food and I would be left hungry. She was forever worried about me going hungry.

My great grandma and I used to walk a long distance to Omungwelume so that she would receive her pension. Because she had a problem with her eyes, she was not totally blind but she could hardly see properly. I used to lead her by a walking stick holding it on one end and she held it on the other end while I was in front. We truly walked shoulder to shoulder and hand by hand. I was my great grandmother's right hand and she was my left hand. We were there for each other in good days as well as in bad days. I was my great grandmother's hand to hold and a shoulder to lean on day and night as well as far and near distances. We give each other's hands to hold and shoulders to lean on.

I still remember, since I was the only child in the house I never left my great grandma all alone unattended. I was always there on her first call on my name. She died knowing that she could always depend on me. In actually fact, when I came to live with my great grandma I was only three years. She played not only grandma role but equally a motherly role. I was still a baby therefore she was my mother too. I thank her for all she has done for me until I grew up to be on my own. I get the feeling it was not easy for her. In a way I thank my great grandma because it was due to my early exposure and responsibilities that I learned to be more responsible in life. I did not only become responsible but she nurtured me to be a disciplined and resilient child.

My great-grandmother passed on the year 1991 when I returned from Zambia, it was a sad moment for me. In fact when I returned back in the country I found her admitted in hospital. I remember when I was taken to visit her in the hospital, I found her very sick. She died the following day after my visit. It was a bad news. She was super strong with a heart of a warrior. I salute you my great grandma. I am forever grateful to you for taking care of me when my mother was unhealthy to do it, continue resting in peace great grandma.

To my grandfather: My paternal grandfather's death was equally a devastating moment. My grandfather and I were very close friends. That was the man who gave me a father. Gabriel Taukeni was his name. He was nicknamed *Shiti* by his peers for his love of working in the woods. In my home language Oshikwanyama *Shiti* simply means a stick. Apparently my grandfather always had a stick in his hand and that is how he got the nickname *Shiti*.

My late grandfather taught me many good lessons in life. I used to visit him several times when I was down or when I achieved something in life for example passing a grade, buying a car or a house and many more. He blessed me with his kind words and his teaching. He was my best counselor and a life guard. When the news came of his passing in 2004 I felt like my other part of life was gone. It was a big loss to me and my children. My grandfather was a socialist and a community practitioner on spiritual, cultural and traditional issues. He spent most of his active youth life working in mines during the period of 1950s to late 1960s in Upington, a town located in the Northern Cape province of South Africa.

Growing up I knew my grandfather as a spiritual teacher. When I was a small boy, I used to attend his church services at his home. He built his own church made of fresh woods. I enjoyed his Sunday services in his fresh and well-naturally ventilated church. Even chairs in his church were made of wood. Listening to him preaching was a life changing. He was blessed with preaching skills and a golden voice. He studied the bible very well.

He served as cultural and traditional teacher in the community as well. Most people used to consult him on issues related to the spiritual, cultural and traditional. He was really good and he served his clients exceptionally well. Whenever I was not quite clear about what to do in life I would go and seek his opinion. My grandfather was a good listener, I think that was his strong attribute to work with so many people very well. When I needed a friend to listen to my problem, it was my grandfather I ran to and talked to. I knew he would sit me down and listen to me. Without him alive I know I lost a great friend with a good listening ear. That makes me miss him even more.

Equally so, my grandfather was a humble man and peaceful. I never heard of him quarreling with anybody in my entire life. We lived in the same village and I used to spend most of my time at his house but I never saw him angry. I also cannot remember him making jokes though, I think he was a busy man yet he remained loving and caring. When he was talking to us his grandchildren he was always direct and on point. He was a man of few words.

I remember when I was complaining one day during one of our family gatherings saying "Oh grandpa you finished too soon while we are still eagerly waiting to hear more from you." He always remembered what he advised you on before and he never liked repeating himself. I used to miss him a lot when I was far from him, especially when I was at school. Every time I came back home during my school holidays I made sure I first paid my grandfather a visit.

Also, he was the best hand man we had in the family and overall in the village. He was good with his hands, the best craftsman. The way he used to build and decorate his house with the wood it would leave you speechless. He was simply talented. He enjoyed most of his time working on his yard fence *(ongubu) everyday, right through the year.* He was always at his fence, he never got tired of working on it. He would fix the fence such that even the air could not go through it, until it was perfectly and neatly done. My grandfather played a significant role in my life for which I will always remember him. He prayed for me and blessed my house. My grandfather was an old man but he was not that old yet to leave us. He died in his hospital bed looking very strong after a short illness. Continue resting in peace grandpa.

To all my late family relatives: I would like to pay homage to all my late family relatives. My paternal grandmother Ottilie Tuutale Ndilimeke Leevi who died before we were born. I would like to thank her for giving us a wonderful father and aunt.

My maternal grandfather whom I could not meet in person, I thank him for giving me a mother. My late aunt Saima, my only mother's sister I thank her for healing my stomach pain when I was sick in her care and for all the efforts she made to ensure that I was well to write my Grade 12 examination.

My late maternal uncles, Shiini and Mwaetako who took care of my mother when she was sick. I met uncle Shiini taking my mother to the hospital on his bicycle one day. I thank him for having done that for my mother. Uncle Mwaetako was a kind hearted man, he supported me when I was in secondary school giving me clothes and shoes to wear. Whenever he came from Cape Town where he was working he would send people that I should go and see him. I thank him for the support. May their souls rest in eternal peace.

APPENDIX I

Photographs

Simon's father George Mandume Taukeni

Simon's family: *Meme* Fransina, children: Tangi, Tanga and Tunga

Simon and his daughter Tangi teaching her how to swim, 2010

Simon and his first born daughter Fransina Netumbo

Simon and UNAM BEd class of 1999 proud to
be in their final 4th Year, Windhoek

Simon, Tangeni, Kassy and Kamati during BEd
graduation, Safari Windhoek, 2000

Simon, Samkage, Ruben, Nox, Supervisor Prof.
Rembe and Mpofu at UFH, 2009

Simon talking about research with: Ruben, Mbele,
Nox and Henry at UFH Alice, 2010

Some coaching moments

Simon and Soccer Boys Team from Tonateni Centre in Oshakati, 2014

Simon and under 12 Soccer Boys Team at
Windhoek International School, 1998

Simon Presented with a gift by Mrs. Katau after his motivation speech
at Ohangwena Teachers Annual Conference in Ongwediva, 2013

Simon (center) Paulus Noa (left) and local Counselor
at Oshigambo Teachers' Annual Conference, he was
presenting about Inclusive Education, 2014

Simon at UFH doing his PhD,

2011 Simon at Student
center doing MEd, 2008

Simon enjoying his love of reading at UFH
Study Office in Alice Campus, 2009

07/05/2011 11:18

When Simon was about to send his PhD project to external
examiners in Postgraduate study office, 2011

Prof. Rembe (Simon's supervisor) reading Simon's short biography
during PhD graduation ceremony at UFH Alice Campus hall, 2012

Simon facilitating a training for UNAM Teaching and
Learning Improvement Unit at Neudam Campus, 2013

Simon presenting a message of support at Tsengiwe in
Cala, South Africa during World AIDS day, 2014

Simon presenting at 16 Days of Activism of Women and Children against Abuse at UFH Staff Center in Alice Campus, 2015

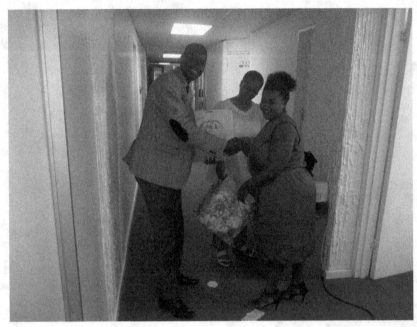

Simon was presented a present from his secret pal by Ms. Penny while Mrs. Giyose was witnessing from UFH Nursing Sciences Department, 2014

Simon and Sr. Wilma getting donations for Orphan
children from a local shop in Oshakati, 2012

Simon presented with a gift by Prof. Eunice Seekoe in East London,
South Africa after facilitating the conference session, 2014

Simon his first year of teaching at Oshimwaku Combined school, 2000

Simon receives an umbrella and raincoat from Mrs. Regina at Tonateni
Catholic AIDS Action where he serves as a volunteer, 2013

Simon at Oshoopala center in Oshakati serving
Orphans and other vulnerable children, 2014

Simon encouraging learners at Oshimwaku Combined
School, Veronika, Naemi and Veronika, 2001

Simon doing bereavement counselling during a colleague's
death announcement at Tonateni Center, 2014

Simon touching lives sponsoring a surprising Christmas Party
for Security officers at UNAM HP Campus, 2013

Simon with his young cousin Samuel Taukeni donated and handed over the sport supplies to Sr. Wilma for Orphans and Other Vulnerable Children at Tonateni Catholic AIDS Action in Oshakati, 2011

Given my chicken as a gift by a colleague Ms. Christy, 2015

Presented with a Bible and Hymn *Simanekeni Karunga* by Sr. Wilma

Simon was recently given a surprise shock of his life when a
small girl came looking for him brought with her a big chicken
as a token of community appreciation of his service to the
orphans and vulnerable children, Tonateni Centre, 2016.

Simon showing off his Soccer skills at UNAM Soccer Stadium, 2002

Simon with UNAM Rangers F.C at UNAM main Campus, 1998

MY CONTRIBUTION
TO HUMANITY

My contribution to humanity are things I do freely and passionately to bring about positive change in the lives of my fellow human beings. I make a contribution through counseling and guidance assistance, provision of psychosocial support and sport activities. I have counseled many students who were addicted to alcohol and drugs and after they had consulted me they experienced a positive change which led them not to use alcohol and drugs anymore.

There were some students who were on the verge of dropping out due to having failed many subjects during their studies at the university. But after they had consulted my office they started seeing a better way of coping. Most of them ended up graduating and that was an exciting moment to see a student graduating who was so depressed and about to drop out. I spoke to some of the student who were arrested and jailed for committing crime. After I spoke to them, they ended up changing their lives, stopped doing crime and became productive citizens. Most of these students are today university graduates and that is where the joy of my contribution to humanity is measured and appreciated.

I have also worked with many orphan and other vulnerable children in my community to support them emotionally, psychologically, socially, spiritually and physically. Specifically, I have been there for orphan and other vulnerable children to listen to their fears, coping mechanisms, how they were doing in life and guided them to strive for a better future. Most of these children regard me as a 'father of the children' a term they used in my home language as '*Tate wuunona*'.

In most cases I provided school uniforms and other basic needs to orphans, because growing up as an orphan myself I understand very well that life can be really difficult sometimes. I play a significant role in the academic lives of orphan children by giving them extra classes especially as a volunteer at Catholic AIDS Action, Tonateni Center in Oshakati. We had many children who were finding it difficult to cope academically which was clearly visible in their school term end reports. I usually targeted the children with ungraded and failed subjects. There were those who became really good and even passed their grades with good marks. I am a humanitarian, that is what and how I was born to be.

I also provide training on psychosocial support to parents and caregivers to ensure that children are supported in terms of food, clothing, schooling, national documents and church, mainly functions such as baptism and confirmation. My training on psychosocial support covers children's rights and different types of child abuse. Talking from experience many caregivers did not have knowledge about the rights of children and different forms and signs of child abuse and neglect. It is my hope to continue making a small difference in the lives of orphan and other vulnerable children.

MY MESSAGE TO ORPHAN CHILDREN

If one or both of your parents are dead and left you all alone as an orphan child to struggle in this world my message to you is that you are not alone. I was there and I went through that and look at what I have to achieved. Remain focused and keep doing the right things and your success will come. Look at my story from how I survived from the day I was born where nobody ever imagined that a poor mother would give birth to a surviving child. I was even baptized the same day I was born because my family felt that I would die anytime sooner or later after birth, it never happened I survived it. I am still a healthy and strong successful PhD holder today.

It is my hope that you get an opportunity to read my entire story where you can read that I grew up in the village, refugee camps, poor and orphaned but I never gave up on my dreams of becoming successful and I worked hard to be on top of my game. I am still working hard and this book is a testimony. I have made it with flying colors and you too can make it.

As an orphan child you may feel that without having rich and well to do parents and family one cannot achieve anything. I can honestly say that is a lie and a bad excuse. I tell you with my open heart from my personal experience that my parents were all dead and buried but I achieved my dreams without them supporting me. You may want to know how I did it, first you must have faith and secondly you must work hard. That is all I needed to do and God had sent his Angels to show me the way and support.

By angels here I refer to people who supported me not because I was their family member but those who looked at me and God had touched their hearts to decide to support me. For example my grandmother was one of my Angels, that Samaritan teacher who gave my grandmother money so that I could pay my grade 12 examination that woman was our Angel. My God mother Mrs. English at the University of Namibia who understood my poverty situation to make it easy for me so that I could write my examination until I graduated to becoming a teacher, she was indeed my Angel. And all God's people who contributed in a positive way towards my achievement and to have a better life are equally my Angels. And you too God has already prepared your Angels to support you so that you achieve your goals. Perhaps I can be your potential Angel if this book touches your heart and gives you a message of hope.

I can also tell you that there are bad people who will work hard to put you down and fight against your success. I too have faced many of those bad in my life but I left them, I ran away as fast as I could and moved on to be with more positive and good people. You need to do the same, please run away from bad people. Some of them will come to tell you that let us go kill and steal, say no to them and they must leave you alone. Some of them will come to tell you let us go drink alcohol and use drugs to forget about our situation, do not believe them. If you are an orphan child never think of crime, alcohol and drugs abuse. Doing those things will not help you achieve anything tangible and everlasting. You have to believe me on that, remain a disciplined child and stay away from all social evils.

I grew up very poor, orphaned and in refugee camps but I never committed any crime of any kind as an excuse for my situation. I still hate alcohol and drugs up to this day. I found those things a waste of time. Maybe I am far from you at the moment look closely at successful people in your community, you will find that people of good social standing and character do not engage themselves in social evils. Stay clean and remain focused to achieve your dreams. I wish you success in whatever you are doing. May God bless you and may He sends His Angels to support and show you the way.

MY BELIEF ON THE BEAUTY OF LIFE

I believe there is a great Law of Attraction of which all things in life are attracted toward each other in an undefined way and to me that force of attraction is the beauty of life. I believe that there are two forces of the law of attraction, the Positive and Negative. The beauty of life is that Positive attracts Negative in all spheres of life.

Life is the magnet and that is the beauty of it all. I believe that everything on earth has the potential of life in it. I believe that INNOVATION, DESIRE, and WILLPOWER create the beauty of life. To break it down I would say we all have an inborn potential to bring the best out of life. One can use innovation, desire and willpower to create a hit song of the year and to me that is the beauty of life. Like me, I used my innovation, desire to write, willpower to commit and the end result is this beautiful story in the book. This is what I believe is the beauty of life.

I believe in self-love. I sincerely believe that if one does not love oneself he/she cannot love other people. Beauty of life is when you stop comparing oneself to other people or when you allow others to compare you with the other people. Beauty of life is when you are being yourself at all times. It is when one discovers his or her true self. We all have what is called the "I" meaning individuality. The "I am" is the one that makes me different from the rest, for instance I am unique in my individuality. Do you know your I am?

This question takes us back to what I said earlier about innovation, desire and willpower. We all can be the best we can, not as a copy of one another but with our own innovation, desire and willpower. Simply put, my innovation is my own alone, my interest is uniquely in my heart and soul and my commitment defines my ability to pursue my God given potential. All these elements put together form a character and a personality. Doing so, this is how one discovers his or her individuality. In the end that is how the beauty of life manifests itself. As a reader reading my life story you may still have questions regarding the three elements namely innovation, desire and willpower. Let me make them clear without going into detail of their original meanings or what they mean in the academic world.

I use my own belief system to unpack them as follows: I believe that when I talk of INNOVATION I am referring to one's technical knowhow and skills to create something from nothing. The beauty of life is seen from the innovation that created the product, meaning that the combination of knowhow, skills and action applied to give life to the product leaves a trademark of the creator.

I equally believe that DESIRE is the interest or the ambition to do something. The beauty of life is appreciated or not appreciated considering the desire demonstrated in the process of creating the product. And finally WILLPOWER is the amount of energy and commitment one puts in during the process of creating a product. The product can be anything as an end result or an outcome of the three elements. Therefore I believe that we are all born with a potential of innovation, desire and willpower to do something in our best unique way and that is the beauty of life.

Before I leave this section, let me tell you what my philosophy of life is all about. I feel that my belief on the beauty of life is directly informed by my philosophy of life. I believe in gaining knowledge and that knowledge is my strength to know the difference between what to do and what not to do. I also believe that we see life from the way we think. What I choose to think about myself and about life becomes true for me.

As human beings we create our life from the way we think. Louise. L. Hay puts it well "If I want to believe that life is lonely and that nobody loves me, then that is what I will find in my world." I sincerely believe that our thoughts we think and the words we use create the life we live and believe. Life is just a thought and a thought can be changed if it is not what we want. Still, wrong thoughts lead to wrong choices therefore wrong actions and wrong consequences. The opposite is true.

HOW I WOULD LIKE TO BE REMEMBERED

L et us face the truth, once we finish our assignment on earth to serve God's purpose we will die and go back to the Creator. Once that happens we would have left a legacy of how we would like to be remembered. I want current and next generations to remember me that there was a poor village boy known as Simon George who lived his life honestly and purposefully. I want to be remembered as a poor village boy and a refugee boy who despite all odds became a university graduate to earn a PhD in a record of two years. Chances are higher that I could be the first person in the history of Eengendjo SSS to earn a PhD degree. I often count my blessings when God chose me out of all the people in my community to get ahead in life.

I want people to remember me as an ordinary poor boy who never stopped learning and studying. As a boy who made a solidarity contribution with other brave freedom fighters who brought independence to Namibia at a very tender age of thirteen years. I believe some people are born great, some achieve more to be great and some work hard to become the greatest. I want to be remembered as one of those who worked hard to achieve my God given purpose to become the greatest in my own right.

I have faced many life challenges but honestly speaking I had never given up on my dreams not even one bit. It is my hope that people would remember me as somebody who never gave up despite all odds. There is an important aspect of my life I hope people picked it up, my love for sport. I love sport so much that I formed a soccer team called Future Boys Football Club in my village. When I started that football club my ambition was mainly to help me stay away from social evils and I succeeded. I hope people in my Omundudu village will remember me as an ordinary boy playing his soccer with small boys from the village.

Even at Eengendjo Secondary School my friends and I formed a soccer team called Young Boys Football Club. That team was comprised of mainly young boys studying at Eengendjo SSS and who were not playing in the school's senior soccer team. My soccer nickname was Hammer.

I enjoyed my time being a player of Young Boys Club. We used to be a good team. We challenged and won many soccer competitions. We were a very tough team. I can say our purpose to form the club was really to help us remain focused in our education. We used to have soccer meetings where we advised each other that we should not engage ourselves in social evils but to stay away from societal problems and we succeeded, most of us have good careers and better jobs.

Growing up I was never perfect but I lived my life honestly and purposefully. Wherever I stayed I mostly enjoyed peace, love, kindness, honest and fairness. I think that anyone who knows me will remember me talking about those qualities. I know very well that I was never seen at alcohol drinking places like bars or sheeben and things of that kind which attract most young people to have fun but I was always enjoying going to church. I started going to church at a very tender age. At that time Omundudu was still under Endola church, so I used to walk to go and listen to the word of God at Endola Elcin church.

Sometimes I asked to join *Tate* Aron in his beautiful car to and from church as our neighbor. I remember him asking me always after church that: "Simon George tell us the biblical readings that were read today at church and their meaning?" That was the question I was always asked by *Tate* Aron and his wife *Meme* Ndamononghenda after every Sunday service. To tell the truth I remembered everything from the name of the book, chapter, verse and what the pastor was preaching about.

I used to have an old bible and I remember *Meme* Ndamonoghenda used to tease me about my old bible, "Simon *shiveli* I will buy you a new bible one day soon." And she laughed. For me that was one of the most memorable highlights of my life of which people should remember me about, me and my old bible.

I used to see most young boys at my village drinking *otombo* and other traditional beers, I stayed away from those kind of young people. I should be remembered as a boy who never wasted his time with non-productive things. I came to learn that my life was saved by two things namely playing sport and going to church. These two events played a significant role and contributed positively to my life. If it were not for them I do not know what I could have achieved. Perhaps we all need to identify things we love to do and yet keeping us focused to achieve our dreams. For me it was sport and the love of God.

I am a very spiritual person, emotional and easy to cry. I think losing all my parents and great parents left me with so much grief and amount of emotions. I already mentioned my love for going to church. I should then now tell the readers my favorite hymn songs in *Ehangano* as follows: 73, 118, 180, 192, 331, 332, 483 and 562. My first hymn song I learned and memorized was 382 *Yoga ndj', Omuwa*. In *Simanekeni Karunga* hymn book my favorite song is 100. Remember to sing these songs at my funeral when my days in this world are over.

I love reading the Bible as well. My favourite readings people should remember me for are: Psalm 23:1-8; Psalm 40:1-17; Philippians 2: 1-11 and James 3: 13-18. The principle of scripture that guided my personal and professional life is written in Romans 12: 6-21. Everything I did and do was based on these words of God.

Equally important, remember all other good things I committed my time towards the betterment of humankind as a contribution without asking anything in return. You can also remember me that I wrote this book you are reading. Turn to the next page to read how I thank God who is the man behind all my success.

THANKING GOD,
THE FATHER

It is one thing to ask God the father for the guidance and blessings, it is another to say thank you God for your blessings that you have bestowed upon me. I was privileged to go through life and gained blessings in the form of education, beautiful children, a job, shelter to sleep, food on my table, clothes to wear, a friend I can trust and my good neighbors.

All these could not have been possible without the power and mercy of God. There were days in my life where I never knew how I would survive difficult situations facing me but God has always been there for me to show me the best way possible. I went through so much in life but God has never left me alone, his Angels were all over me to support and save my life. As I come to the end of this book of my life I would like to finally thank the man with whom I owe my life and all the blessings. Thank you God the father for everything I have in life. With all blessings from God, next page I talk more about how I see myself.

HOW I SEE MYSELF

Let me take time to put it on record of how I see myself and what type of a man I am. People like to talk for others and they seem to think that they know them better. The list of who I see myself is endless but for the benefit of this book let me highlight my main traits as follows:

Father

There is nothing more important in life than the love of my children. The gap my father left when he went to be with the Lord has made me realize that it is important to be the best father I can be to my children. The thing I miss most in life is the love of my father. My father is gone but I feel like wanting to see and talk to him nearly every day. As a father myself I love my children very much. I am the best father my children can ask for from the day they were born until the end of time. My children know that I will support the choices they make in life and they know that I will never limit them. I see myself as a father who wants his children to be the best they can be in life.

Barrier breaker

I might be born in the environment of defeat and in mediocrity family but I set new records by breaking the barriers to become a successful story. I have been setting new records and broke many barriers in my entire life.

Remember that I was born to be a barrier breaker, don't forget that my family did not accept the idea that my poor mother would give birth to a healthy child, me. I broke that crazy barrier of thinking and my mother set a record. I was born healthy and still I am healthier writing this book. My father was a wonderful man, very successful in his own right. He went to school and became educated but not as far as I did. I broke the new record and became the first man to get the highest qualification in Taukeni family. I was the first to get a PhD at the age of 38 in my family. Let us see who will be the next in my family to break that record.

It is true that I was born by a poor mother who never went to school in her life. But I broke a new record, my mother just gave birth to an educated man that is me breaking the barriers of thinking. I am a barrier breaker, a go getter and an achiever. If you read my entire story you can see that I could not have achieved what I have achieved if I were not a barrier breaker. There were many barriers. Some of the barriers were intentionally put up to stop me by some people in authority but in the end I got what I wanted, meaning I broke their barriers. Some of the barriers were naturally in my way due to my family background and poverty situation but I never folded my arms to wait for things to happen on their own. I dreamed big and I worked hard daily until God sent His Angels to help me break the barriers.

One thing you should know about me and why it is easy for me to break barriers is that I studied psychology, I understand people behavior. In order to break the barrier I need to avoid reconditioning my mind of negative things people are saying about me. That's why earlier on I said I never cared about what people say about me. My life is my life and it is up to me to get it where I want it to go. If I do a mistake along the way, so be it, I am just a human being moving my life forward. I also understand very well people around you can set barriers for you. I never allowed that to happen and I will never allow anybody to tell me that I am not good enough for this and that. It is up to me to fix what needs to be fixed.

Dreamer

I am a life time dreamer. I believe in my dreams. Dreams help me achieve and define what I want to become or what I don't want to become. I see that picture of me first before I get my destiny right. Everything I achieved in life I first dreamed about me achieving them. I am not just a dreamer and it ends up there, I am also a philosopher too. Anyone can dream of any kind of life and leave it there, as just a dream. I am not like that, I am therefore a dreamer and a philosopher.

Philosopher

I create my own world and live happily thereafter in my imagination. It starts first with a dream and I turn it into a reality to create my life out of that imagination. Nothing is a surprise to me, I first had it in my imagination before I make it to happen. I dream how I want my life to be and I follow that dream taking all choices and resources available to create the life I want. I have been doing just like that seeing myself in imagination and creating the reality out of that imagenary picture. Everything I became I first saw that in my imagination. I am a philosopher, I see my life before it happens.

Before my dad went to be with the Lord, I first saw myself without a father and I needed to do something before I become a homeless boy. I bought my house in the same year my dad died. I had that imagination of him leaving and of me not having a place I call home, that was me the philosopher.

Lifelong learner

I believe in the lifelong learning. Learning is part of life. I cannot see myself surviving if I am not learning. I learn to live. I learn to cope in life. I learn to know. I learn to understand everything and everybody in life.

Forgiver

I know very well that I am not perfect, I do a lot of mistakes. But I forgive myself for the mistakes I made so that I create a space for peace to come in my heart. I forgive myself by letting go and move on. Equally so as a child of God I forgive people who treat me badly. In most cases I walk away from toxic people and toxic environment, I just walk away peacefully to focus on my destiny. Toxic people are like a poison and a virus, I never stay near them and give them time to infect me. I just run really fast away from them. I also never waste my energy to keep on holding to the past mistakes or to what people did say or do to me. I need my energy to do more exciting things for my life. Time is so limited to waste on the mistakes of the past because they can spoil the good things of the present. I just hate living in the past and I know for sure that I will never allow that to happen to my peaceful life. I am truly a forgiving man, peaceful and most favored. By being a forgiving man I don't mean that I am a stupid person who does not care about ill-treatment and evil people. On contrary I do care a lot because I am a firm believer in a nonviolent society. I also believe in inclusive society where every human being should be treated fairly, respected, valued, listened to and given equal opportunity to live happily and freely with other fellow human beings.

MY FINAL WORDS AND PROMISE

My final words are that if you are a village boy or girl or perhaps an older person who grew up very poor in the village, this book could have taken you back down memory lane. As I come to the end of my book I have a strong feeling to shout really aloud and say get up and do something good for your life. Do not wait for tomorrow to come, tomorrow never comes and time is going.

Start like me with baby steps. Writing this book I started word by word then sentence by sentence, sentences became paragraphs and paragraphs became sections. At the time I had my sections I started emailing the publishers in order to compare the publication costs. Before I knew it I was writing this section: MY FINAL WORDS AND PROMISE. I was like wait again, how did I get here so fast? I had all those stories to tell that filled up all pages into a finished product called my autobiography and I still have more stories left to tell and more journeys to walk. If I were to wait for tomorrow to start writing I could not have my life stories in a book today because tomorrow is still yet to come.

I have a feeling you know how I feel about myself right now, let me save your time from guessing. I am proud of myself that my story is out there in the world to inspire and teach people that we all can be the best we want to be and we all have a story to tell the world. Throughout the book I referred to many people only by their first names to ensure some privacy and I only used full names for people who are my immediate family members and people who are already public figures.

My final promise is that God willing, I will publish my second part of this life journey that would cover my life from the age of 42 to 60 and it is my hope that you and I will still be alive to read more about my life to touch you and inspire you even further. Thank you for reading my life story.

Reflection and feedback

Finally, it is my hope that I fulfilled my promise to inspire you and give you courage to go on with your life. After finished reading my story which I hope you did, let me now leave you with this question to reflect on. On the grading scale out of 10: Did I take the limited opportunities presented to me and utilize them successfully, how much can you score me? _____/10.

Example: One can be given a study scholarship but ended up failing or dropping out.

If you would like to send my score please feel free to send it to my email: staukeni@gmail.com I will appreciate for the feedback that you read my book.

APPENDIX II

Autobiographical Profile Of Simon George Taukeni

Born in December 23, 1973 in Omundudu in the Ohangwena Region, Namibia. His parents are late George Mandume Taukeni and Maria Mwaifanange Kalola. He has five paternal siblings, Appolos, Ottilie, Abner, Aloys and Alex and one maternal sister Eveline Namutenya Nghishiivali. Simon George is blessed with four children: Fransina Netumbo, Tangi-Hope, Tanga-Happy and Tunga-Home Georgia.

Education
Omundudu Combined School (Pre & Primary Education) (1981-1987)
Kwanza Sul SWAPO Education Center (Primary Education), Angola (1988-1989)
Nyango Education Center (Junior Secondary Education), Zambia (1989-1990)
Eengendjo SSS (Senior Secondary Education) Namibia (1991-1994)
Bachelor of Education degree, University of Namibia (1996-2000)
Specialized Post-Graduate Diploma in Special Education, UNAM (2002-2004)
Masters of Education, University of Fort Hare, South Africa (2008-2009)
Doctor of Philosophy in Education, University of Fort Hare (2010-2012)
Post-Doctoral Research Fellowship, University of Fort Hare (2014-2015)
Masters in Public Health, University of Fort Hare, (2015-2017)

Work

Kohler Corrugated Company, Walvis Bay Namibia (1995)
Epundi Primary School (1995)
Windhoek International School (1997-1999)
Oshimwaku Combined School (2000-2003)
Iipumbu Senior Secondary School (2003-2004)
Ongwediva College of Education (2004-2010)
University of Namibia Hifikepunye Pohamba Campus (2011-2014)
University of Fort Hare (2014- 2015), South Africa
Catholic AIDS Action Tonateni Centre (2012-Present)
Namibia College of Open Learning (Oshimwaku 2002-3, Iipumbu SSS 2004,
Ongwediva Control 2005 and Ongwediva Head Office 2015)
University of Namibia Rundu Campus (2016- current)

Languages

Simon George speaks Oshikwanyama (mother tongue) and English.
He has basic vocabularies in Afrikaans, Portuguese and IsiXhosa

Professional focus area

Educational Psychology and Public Health

Expertise and specialization areas

Psychosocial support, Guidance and counseling, Special Education, Educational
Research, Health Research: Epidemiology, Advanced Epidemiology,
Biostatistics
Economics and Physical Education

Sports interest

Future Boys F.C. (Founder and Player -1992 -2000)
Young Boys F.C. (Co-Founder and Player 1992- 1994)
Tough Guys F.C. (Player 1996-1997)
UNAM Rangers F.C. (Player 1998-1999)
Netball (Coach-2000-2004)
Volleyball (Coach 2006-2010)
Tennis and Squash (Fan)
Arsenal F.C. (England, Fan)
Real Madrid (Spain, Fan)

Awards
Bursary and Scholarship
- Namibian Government Student Bursary (Bachelor of Education degree – 1996- 1999)
- Supervisor-linked Scholarship (Masters in Education degree 2008-2009)
- Supervisor-linked Scholarship (Doctor of Philosophy 2010-2011)
- Supervisor-linked Scholarship (Post-Doctoral Fellowship 2014-2015)
- South African National and Provincial Department of Health Scholarship (Masters degree in Public Health 2015-2017)

I was once like you, have faith for a better tomorrow!